SAVANNAH RENAISSANCE

SAVANNAH RENAISSANCE

Best wishes
Lee and Emma Adler

Lee and Emma Adler

Wyrick & Company
Charleston

Published by Wyrick & Company
Post Office Box 89
Charleston, SC 29402

Book design by Sally Heineman

Printed and bound in the United States of America

ISBN 0 -941711-69-2

The authors and publisher would like to thank the
following people and institutions for the use of
photographs and illustrations in this book:

Leopold Adler II Collection
Joseph Byrd & Associates
Grant Compton
Eric DeLony
Daniel L. Grantham, Jr.
Historic Savannah Foundation
Massie Heritage Interpretation Center
Savannah College of Art & Design
University of Georgia Hargett Library
Williams Studio

CONTENTS

FOREWORD

In the 1960s, those cities in the vanguard of the historic preservation movement each had one singular and strong leader, a visionary who relentlessly pursued a mission of an all-encompassing policy for his or her community. No historic building was to be demolished; not one historic property was to be altered to its detriment. In Savannah, that one person was Lee Adler, abetted by his fully engaged and ever-pleasant wife, Emma.

This retrospective is their story of the early years of the "Battle for Savannah." In the '50s and '60s the business leadership envisioned a "new and progressive city" like Jacksonville or Atlanta. Lee Adler saw Savannah's future differently.

Using business practices and promoting the economic benefits of historic preservation, Adler led a small but determined band of preservationists to take risks in the then-decimated downtown real estate market. By acquiring debt, leveraging loans, pledging collateral and raising funds, he demonstrated, time and time again, a keen ability to wrest a historic property away from the disaster of demolition. With Marshall Row's dramatic rescue—quickly following the saving of the Davenport House—he demonstrated a strategy that was ultimately successful in protecting the then-largest collection of historic buildings of any downtown in the nation.

Often, buying at a premium and selling at a loss required a disciplined real estate policy that the fledgling Historic Savannah Foundation dutifully followed, emboldened by Adler's sheer power of will. Sticking to its principle of not selling at a profit, and replenishing the Revolving Fund by charitable fund-raising, the Foundation slowly but surely gained recognition within the community as a bona fide real estate operation.

The preservation record during the 20-year period of 1955–1975 is now even harder to imagine. When first-time visitors see Savannah today, it is nearly incomprehensible that forty years ago the historic fabric of the city was so fragile. Now, upon reflection, one can find very little of old Savannah's physical plant in the heart of the city that has not been touched, influenced, and made better by the Adlers' work over these decades. Although the Save the Bay effort and the later Savannah Landmark programs had some setbacks, on balance, old Savannah exists today as witness to the creative leadership that was the Adlers'.

I learned how to keep old buildings standing from Lee Adler. Countless others nationwide have as well. Today, the Old City's beauty of heritage is an Adler legacy. But so are Adler-inspired examples in cities and towns across this vast nation which have chosen historic preservation to be an important redevelopment and economic stimulus tool, not just for sustainability, but for quality growth and sound development as well.

J. Reid Williamson, Jr.
President/CEO
Historic Landmarks Foundation of Indiana, Inc.

PREFACE AND ACKNOWLEDGMENTS

We have been involved with the task of creating this account of Savannah's renaissance since 1996, when our friend Jim Fitch suggested that we undertake the project and gave us a substantial grant to make his idea a reality. We owe him special thanks. The *New York Times* characterized Jim Fitch as "an architect whose writings and teaching helped transform historic preservation from a dilettante's pastime into a vigorous, broadly based cultural movement." Lee was a lecturer for years in Jim's graduate program in restoration and preservation at Columbia University. We would see him at annual conferences of the National Trust for Historic Preservation, at which he often gave a riveting presentation. We regret that we were unable to complete the task before Jim's death in 2000 at age ninety. We are also indebted to his widow, Martica Sawin, president of the James Marston Fitch Charitable Trust, as well as to trust member and friend Eric DeLony.

Connie and Pete Wyrick, good friends and fine publishers in Charleston, South Carolina, deserve the next recognition. After reading a first draft in 1997—an ambitious effort to create a chronological record of Historic Savannah Foundation's goals and accomplishments year by year from 1955 through 1968—the Wyricks suggested a narrative approach on a personal level. By late 1997, we had drafted such a narrative.

Dr. Elizabeth Lyon, Georgia's recently retired state historic preservation officer, also a friend, used our material in an article she prepared for the National Trust for Historic Preservation's publication *Forum*, an educational component of the trust's annual conference in Savannah in 1998. We appreciate her interest and support.

Liz Lyon suggested that we ask Jane Powers Weldon in Atlanta to review the manuscript as an editor. Jane's tactful and gentle professional assistance has been constant from 1998 to the present. During our pleasant association we have become friends, and we give Jane well-deserved credit for shepherding the project to its completion.

Thanks go also to our long-time friend and dedicated preservationist Elizabeth Lattimore Reiter for her constructive suggestions. Richard Moe, president of the National Trust for Historic Preservation; John Reps, distinguished urban planner from Cornell University; and Arthur Ziegler, president of the Pittsburgh History and Landmarks Foundation, deserve thanks for their

James Marston Fitch, noted architect and preservationist, is flanked by Lee Adler and Frances Edmunds, legendary Executive Director of Historic Charleston Foundation. Jim Fitch, believing the story of Savannah's renaissance to be of national interest, initiated the creation of this book with a grant to the authors from his private foundation.

approval and supportive statements.

We are particularly grateful to J. Reid Williamson, former director of Historic Savannah Foundation and current president and CEO of the Historic Landmarks Foundation of Indiana, for his assistance with the manuscript and for his excellent foreword.

Relying heavily on primary source material, we have tried to include as much detail as possible during the period of our involvement, and we encourage others to write about our city's renaissance from their points of view. We are delighted that Wyrick & Company made our work a reality and give special thanks to Pete Wyrick and his staff for their outstanding assistance with the illustrations.

INTRODUCTION

Savannah, a major port in the southeast, is the seat of the Georgia colony established by the English in 1733. The city's unique town plan at its fulfillment in 1856 featured twenty-four magnificent squares shaded by indigenous trees—pines, live oaks, magnolias, and palmettos—and surrounded by substantial eighteenth- and nineteenth-century buildings. Today, twenty-one squares remain intact.

Savannah's riverfront stretches a mile along the southern bank of the Savannah River where the city was founded at the top of a forty-foot bluff in 1733. From that time, this area has been the main commercial part of the city. This was the early heart of Savannah, a busy port. A flat strip of land lies along the river bank, large enough for docks, a sufficient loading area, and in later days a railroad spur from the main line. The banks of the river were sand, as was the bluff. In early days, merchants conducted their business from low buildings on wharves at the river's edge. Rice, naval stores, and lumber were major exports by 1786, and the new item in Georgia's economy was cotton.

In time, after the invention of the cotton gin in 1793 and the increase in cotton exports, it became necessary to shore up the bluff, move further inland, and erect substantial buildings. Material was at hand in the form of large ballast stones that had been dumped in a quarry across the river. The city faced the bluff with masonry in the early 1840s. In the embankment, the Irish-born architect Charles B. Cluskey built warehouses, the "Cluskey Stores," with arched vaults along the ramps below town level. A row of buildings facing East Bay Street, erected between 1854 and 1858 by John Stoddard, became known as Stoddard's Upper Range. In the 1850s, before the Civil War, the harbor and river were greatly improved, and, with appropriations from national and city governments, much-needed dredging and removal of wrecks that had obstructed the channel since the Revolutionary War were carried out, thus improving the river approaches to the city.

It is widely known that in his march to the sea during the Civil War, General William T. Sherman, instead of burning Savannah, "presented" the city "along with 150 bales of cotton" to President Abraham Lincoln as a Christmas present in 1864. Sherman made his headquarters in the fine mansion on Madison Square offered by its owner, Charles Green, and according to William Harden's *History of Savannah and South Georgia*, the occupation of the city was carried out in an orderly manner with schools, churches, and local businesses open and functioning as soon as possible.

The Upper Ranges along Bay Street became the heart of the cotton trade. In offices in these buildings merchants made their fortunes. The second level on the city side opened on what became known as Factors' Walk. There, under an iron network of bridges and girders, the cotton factors (brokers) would inspect the bales of cotton unloaded from barges and freight cars for purchase and shipment. The center of the cotton trade was an imposing building, the Savannah Cotton Exchange, designed by the nationally prominent architect from Boston, William G. Preston, and completed by 1888. It was here and in Liverpool, England, that international prices were set for cotton.

The cotton era endured throughout the nineteenth century, and during this period the substantial and unique buildings along the riverfront were erected. There was symmetry in the wonderful warehouses, which, after the decline of cotton caused by the boll weevil and competition from other markets, fell into disuse and often disrepair. In the upper stories facing Bay Street, however, businesses established after the cotton era populated the Factors' Walk area and constituted busy commercial institutions of the city. The insurance companies and shipping companies here were an important part of the life of Savannah. The handsome U.S. Custom House, designed by John S. Norris of New York, was active on the southeast corner of Bay Street at Bull Street. Buildings along the south side of Bay Street also housed brokerage businesses. There had been some demolition on this side of Bay Street, and these empty lots were used for parking. Commercial and banking facilities were concentrated around Johnson Square in the heart of the old city, with markets, retail, and entertainment facilities nearby. By the early 1950s the port had expanded farther up the Savannah River.

The city retains a sophisticated, formal urban atmosphere with a European flavor. It is a delight to walk along Bull Street, which runs north-south dividing the old city east from west. The street proceeds from square to square under lush canopies of trees and is lined with graceful and imposing churches whose spires reach skyward above buildings that respect the human scale. The Bull Street squares are accented with monuments in the center section of each. An obelisk in Johnson Square to Nathanael Greene, a Revolutionary War hero, was designed by William Strickland of Philadelphia. A monument in memory of railroad magnate William Washington Gordon is centered in Wright Square. This massive piece with pink marble columns displaced the simple yet dignified burial mound of Tomochichi, the Yamacraw Indian chief who befriended Oglethorpe and the colonists and asked to be buried in the square. Later, the Savannah Town Committee of the National Society of Colonial Dames of America purchased a huge rock of Georgia granite and placed it in a corner of the square in Tomochichi's memory. Farther along, in Chippewah Square, a bronze statue of the colony's founder, James Edward Oglethorpe, is by Daniel Chester French, of Lincoln Memorial fame. There are also monuments in Madison and Monterey Squares to Sergeant William Jasper, an Irish hero during the Revolution, and to Count Casimir Pulaski, a gallant Polish nobleman. Both men fell in the siege of Savannah in 1779.

Though designed long before the advent of the automobile, Savannah's eighteenth-century city plan still works. There have been periodic efforts, in the name of progress, to cut through the squares to ease the flow of traffic. Of course the monuments on Bull Street have made this impossible. But three squares on Montgomery Street, a north-south artery on the west side, were lost. In the 1980s, however, one of these, Franklin Square, was reclaimed.

Savannah's city plan is basically an ancient grid that came from Greece, to Rome, to the British Isles, and then to this country. Its genius lies in its regularly recurring squares, orderly arrangement of house lots with carriage houses and lanes behind them, and rectangular street patterns. This is a disciplined plan. When a building or its set-back changes, the alteration can erode the visual harmony. The discipline of the plan has had an influence through the years on the buildings and has probably played a role in prolonging the life of many of them.

Since the old city of Savannah was developed from 1733 to 1856 by the routine addition of squares, streets, and house lots on land owned by the city, this 2.2-square-mile area had to include all of the diverse uses a city requires. Residences for rich and poor, young and old, are side by side with churches, schools, shops, stores, government buildings, businesses, professional offices and cultural facilities. Churches reflect the influence of many faiths and nationalities. Savannah has been a place where daily life could go on without the automobile, but the plan has accommodated cars while remaining substantially intact.

The city's north boundary is the Savannah River. The Atlantic Ocean inhibits much growth eastward, although inland islands and hammocks above the marshes have been developed at a rapid pace during the last twenty years. The marshes, recognized as an important habitat for marine life, are protected by the state of Georgia. The main growth has been south and west.

Because Savannah is a coastal city, it has had continual contacts up and down the Atlantic seaboard as attested by inscriptions on graves in the Colonial Cemetery, which record births as far away as Rhode Island. The port brings the world to Savannah, whose ethnically diverse population includes inhabitants of African, Chinese, English, French, German, Greek, Irish, Italian, Scottish and Vietnamese descent. There are Christian and Jewish populations with roots going back to the eighteenth century and a more recent Eastern Orthodox population. Hindus and Muslims have a newer presence.

The city's regularly recurring squares that punctuate James Oglethorpe's magnificent grid plan were not given the respect they deserve in the 1950s, although attempts to eliminate them in the name of progress had been repulsed in 1921 by the Society for the Preservation of Parks, formed for this purpose. Efforts to destroy the Habersham Street squares and pave this brick street with asphalt had been thwarted also in 1946. But fire lanes and street-car tracks ran through the squares east and west of Bull Street. Some squares had chain-link fences and were used as playgrounds by downtown schools. One in the northeast section was the site of the city's annual New Year's Eve bonfire. In 1935, the Montgomery Street squares had been cut through to ease the flow of north-south traffic.

Broughton Street was the city's hub for shopping through the 1950s. Department stores, dime stores, specialty shops and movie theaters extended from Abercorn Street to Barnard Street. Along West Broad Street were businesses, clothing stores, movie theaters and confectioneries serving principally Savannah's African American population. Sadly, these businesses closed during the 1960s, and many buildings that housed them on West Broad Street were destroyed. Pictures of West Broad Street in the 1940s and 1950s are exhibited today at the Ralph Mark Gilbert Civil Rights Museum on Martin Luther King, Jr. Boulevard, formerly West Broad Street. The museum exists thanks to the efforts of Westly W. Law, a prominent member of Savannah's African American community who, during the critical years of integration, headed Savannah's NAACP.

In recent years there has been controversy regarding a monument to Savannah's African American community, proposed for River Street and depicting slaves in chains. [At this writing Savannah's city council has approved the monument's design and location; however, the monument is not yet in place.] Excerpts from a presentation to Mayor Floyd Adams on race relations in Savannah, prepared in 1998 in an effort to influence the mood of the proposal, give a feeling about the city's traditions:

"Let us think about race relations in Savannah. This beautiful city has benefitted during its history from fine leadership. James Edward Oglethorpe, founder of Georgia, befriended the Native Americans and was loyal to them; he did not permit slavery and welcomed all who wanted to begin a new life here in the Georgia colony. The colonial motto was 'not for themselves, but for others.' The Georgia colony had a good beginning, and today Georgia is a progressive state boasting the admirable motto 'wisdom, justice, and moderation.'

"Slavery was practiced in Savannah because it had become a part of the agrarian way of life in the southern states. People living today cannot really put themselves in the place of someone living in the eighteenth or nineteenth century, but we know that good and evil coexisted and always will.

"We know that Andrew Bryan, a slave who bought his freedom, became a Baptist minister respected by black and white and that more than a thousand people attended his funeral in downtown Savannah, October 6, 1812. We know too that a public school 'for children of African descent' opened here at the Scarbrough House in 1876, only ten years after the state created a charter for public education."

In the 1950s, some development was beginning on Savannah's south side, but the city's core was still north of DeRenne Avenue, and residents came downtown to shop. The economy, stimulated by World War II, was more vigorous than it had been since the Great Depression. Through the 1930s and 1940s, little change had taken place, except that occasionally a fine building would be saved, and occasionally one would be torn down, giving the resulting vacant area a bombed-out look.

Preservation efforts prior to the 1950s had been mainly those of individuals or patriotic societies. Mary Telfair bequeathed her magnificent mansion designed by the English architect William Jay to the Georgia Historical Society in 1875. The building was opened as a free art museum in 1886. The National Society of Colonial Dames in the State of Georgia acquired the Andrew Low House on Lafayette Square's northwest trust lot for use as its state headquarters in 1928. (Savannah's trust lots were areas set aside for public buildings.)

As a result of a Historic American Buildings Survey (HABS) project, which brought architects and researchers to Savannah in 1934 to record important buildings through photographs and measured drawings, Mayor Thomas Gamble in 1935 created the Savannah Commission for the Preservation of Landmarks. Alida Harper Fowlkes transformed the house of James Habersham, Jr. (1789) into the Pink House, a tearoom and restaurant, in the 1940s, and during this period Mrs. Marmaduke Floyd rescued an old tavern on East Broad Street and christened it the Pirates' House. The Green-Meldrim House on Madison Square, designed by John S. Norris of New York and built in 1850, was saved in 1942 by the Society for the Preservation of Savannah Landmarks, founded by Walter Charlton Hartridge. Today this national landmark is the parish house of St. John's Episcopal Church.

Mr. and Mrs. Hansell Hillyer, in the late 1940s, reclaimed the Trustees' Garden area surrounding the gas works and restored buildings owned by the Savannah Gas Company, of which Mr. Hillyer was president. The site is a ten-acre tract designated by the Trustees of the colony and laid out by General Oglethorpe as an experimental garden. In colonial days, indigo and medicinal plants were cultivated there, and mulberry trees were planted in the hope of developing a silk industry. The historic location and dilapidated wooden buildings served as raw material for the Hillyers, who acquired, restored, and rented properties. They continued until dwelling units and business locations flourished with attractive new Savannah grey brick buildings dotted among the wooden ones to protect them against fires. The accomplishment attracted the attention of television's *Today Show,* on which Mrs. Hillyer described the achievement, but in the late 1940s it gave only indirect impetus to a preservation movement.

It may seem surprising that Savannah had no significant preservation movement until the mid-1950s, whereas Charleston, its neighbor up the coast, had the nation's first historic zoning laws, passed in 1931; an inventory of its historic buildings, *This is Charleston,* published in 1944; and a burgeoning tourist business.

Charleston may have led the country in preserving its architectural heritage, and tourists may have flocked to the city during the winter months, but these facts failed to elicit interest or a competitive spirit in Savannah. While Savannah's historic buildings crumbled, most of Savannah's leaders took no notice. Many Savannahians considered tourists undesirable interlopers and often expressed relief that their city was not disturbed by "Yankee tourists." A satiric poem, "When the Oleanders Bloom Again in Charleston," which deplored Charleston's plight, circulated in Savannah during the 1940s. It began:

> May Day has come, we all rejoice,
> Once more the City's ours;
> The Yankees have departed,
> With the early April flowers.

and continued with the same theme through several verses, one of which read:

> It's a strain to have to be so "Southern,"
> And to be very frank,
> Our gullah intonation
> Is used to gyp the Yank.

The mind-set in Savannah was toward "progress." In the early twentieth century, Savannahians had hailed the fifteen-story Savannah Bank as Savannah's first skyscraper, with no criticism of the fact that the building altered the existing scale on Johnson Square. The business establishment would have traded three squares for a twenty-story building in those days. The downtown was static, even crumbling. In the 1950s, the Telfair Museum seriously considered a move to the south side. As suburbs developed, upper-class families continued to leave their fine homes downtown to build less distinctive, but more comfortable, centrally heated dwellings south of the old city.

Although officials of the National Park Service visited Savannah in 1933 to seek local interest in saving Henry McAlpin's Hermitage (c. 1830), a magnificent plantation house a few miles upriver from the city, they were unsuccessful. Automobile magnate Henry Ford razed the building in 1934 and used its bricks to build his mansion at Richmond Hill. Union Camp Paper Corporation built its plant on the Hermitage site, providing six hundred jobs and a depression-era payroll of $1 million. This was the sort of economic benefit to which Savannah's business establishment aspired.

William Jay's magnificent Habersham House on the southwest trust lot on Orleans Square and the Wetter House on the corner of Oglethorpe Avenue and West Broad Street are prime examples of losses in the 1930s which should never have occurred. The Wetter House could have been saved for $10,000. Half of this amount was offered by a prominent family, but the rest was not raised. The extraordinarily beautiful ironwork from the Wetter House has been used ornamentally as fencing in the downtown area.

In the early 1950s, there was no community-wide recognition of the importance of saving Savannah's irreplaceable eighteenth- and nineteenth-century architecture, but two important mansions were saved by individuals. William Jay's Owens-Thomas House was bequeathed to the Telfair Academy by Miss Margaret Thomas in 1951, and the beautiful birthplace of Juliette Gordon Low, who founded the Girl Scouts of America, was purchased by the National Board of the Girl Scouts in 1953.

Savannah's business establishment considered historic preservation an elitist activity and did not understand the potential value of protecting what could still be saved of the architectural heritage of England's thirteenth colony in America. In fact, in the 1950s the Chamber of Commerce, then housed in William G. Preston's prize-winning Cotton Exchange building, was encouraging the emulation of Jacksonville, Florida, in promoting construction of new, high-rise buildings to bring Savannah into the twentieth century. At this time there was no visitors' bureau, and the Chamber of Commerce, which was closed on weekends, had no concept of a tourist industry that would boost the economy.

We returned from our wedding trip in the fall of 1953 in time to attend a costume ball—the "last hurrah" for Savannah's City Market. We were outraged that this substantial building, which had flourished in Ellis Square since 1888, would be demolished in 1954 to be replaced by a parking garage built by the city with support from downtown merchants to accommodate shoppers and attract them away from a new strip-shopping area on East Victory Drive at Skidaway Road. The demolition of the market would constitute an irreplaceable loss. Unfortunately, there was no organization to reverse this demolition, but this loss served as the catalyst for the creation of Historic Savannah Foundation in 1955.

From 1955 until 1968, during the early years of its existence, Historic Savannah Foundation accomplished seeming miracles in saving what was left of the city's architectural heritage, preserving its streetscapes and many important buildings. But we should mention some tragic losses during these years. The DeSoto Hotel was demolished in 1966 and replaced by the Citizens and Southern Bank and a Hilton hotel. The frivolous reason given by one developer was "the kitchen is too far from the dining room." The imposing, beaux arts Union Station on West Broad Street was replaced by the entrance of Interstate 16 into the city in 1963; a handsome Italianate Masonic lodge on the northwest corner of Telfair Square was replaced in 1972 by a Federal Loan building. At that time Historic Savannah Foundation lacked the influence to protect these three landmarks.

During the 1960s, through the efforts of Historic Savannah Foundation, the only organization working in behalf of preservation, the city and county governments, as well as the business and civic leadership of Savannah, began to understand the economic benefits of historic preservation to this special city. Historic Savannah Foundation brought in many nationally recognized leaders in the field of historic preservation and began a citywide annual celebration of the 1733 founding of Savannah to highlight the city's unique history. The *Savannah Morning News* gave outstanding coverage to all the Foundation's efforts to spread the preservation message. We knew this message was getting across when we walked into City Hall for an appointment with the mayor in 1970 and his assistant greeted us by saying, "What are we going to do about saving the courthouse?" He was referring to William Gibbons Preston's yellow brick building on Wright Square, which was being vacated by the county for a new building on Montgomery Street. We knew that in 1955 no one in the mayor's office would have been concerned and remember thinking that it had taken fifteen years to reach the consciousness of the community. At the state level, Historic Savannah Foundation initiated enabling legislation for a historic zoning ordinance during the 1960s. The citizens of Savannah voted three to one in favor of historic zoning in a public referendum in 1972.

Much has been achieved in the field of preservation in Savannah. The annual meeting of the National Trust for Historic Preservation held here in 1968 can be taken as a benchmark to illustrate significant accomplishment in preservation and to determine the future course of the city in favor of preserving its heritage. The rehabilitation for low-income renters of properties in Savannah's Victorian District, undertaken by Savannah Landmark Rehabilitation Project Inc. in the 1970s–80s, advanced the cause of preservation as well as recognition that the responsible poor who prefer not to live in public housing projects can be good housekeepers. The founding of the Savannah College of Art and Design (SCAD) in 1979 can be taken as a springboard for a second wave of significant preservation in the National Historic District as well as for increased vitality and economic benefit derived from its presence and that of its faculty and students.

In response to a nomination prepared by the City of Savannah's preservation office, in June 1994 the Federal Interagency Panel placed Savannah's city plan, public spaces, and monuments in nomination for inclusion in UNESCO's World Heritage list. Two eminent urban planners, Edmund Bacon of Philadelphia and John Reps of Cornell University, wrote supporting letters. Because of United States regulations which allow the nomination of only public property, no buildings within the area could be included. In spite of the fact that the entire area is a National Historic Landmark District, with many buildings separately designated as landmarks, the nomination was not accepted by the international organization that approves nominations. That the United States sent to Paris Savannah's nomination, as one of two from this country, illustrates the national importance of Savannah's remarkable city plan and what historic preservation has meant to the city.

From the organization of Historic Savannah Foundation in 1955 until the mid-1970s, we were in close contact in the capacity of either officer or member of the executive committee. After the Hyatt Hotel crisis, Lee organized the Savannah Landmark Rehabilitation Project, and Emma served on the board of education and was instrumental in the development of the Massie Heritage Interpretation Center. We have not included a detailed account of Historic Savannah Foundation's activities from the mid-1970s to the mid-1990s, when we were working with other organizations to promote preservation in Savannah. The story of those years remains to be told by others who were involved.

Our approach to this story about our native city and its future is very personal. The book's structure is episodic, with the contents organized by subject. At times we were involved in Savannah's restoration as a team, but at times we acted as individuals in differing capacities. Consequently, in two chapters we have abandoned the plural "we." Emma tells her own story in the chapter "The Massie Heritage Interpretation Center," and Lee describes his in "Savannah Landmark Rehabilitation Project." This account tells how we saw it. From our intimately shared perspective we wrote the book as two and as one.

HISTORIC SAVANNAH FOUNDATION'S EARLY YEARS: STAYING AHEAD OF THE WRECKING BALL

City Market's demolition in 1954 aroused the citizens who came together to form the Historic Savannah Foundation, the preservation organization that achieved meteoric success and national acclaim during the late 1950s through the 1960s. We remember our feelings that evening at the costume ball before the demolition of this monumental building: desperation, a sense of urgency, a need to reverse public opinion. We were relieved when Anna Colquitt Hunter gathered her friends to establish an organization that would prevent further irreplaceable losses. We were delighted that Lee's mother would be among the founders. This group perhaps represented Savannah's last chance to preserve what was left of its architectural patrimony. Prosperity was bringing momentum for change, and this momentum toward "progress" meant the demolition of eighteenth- and nineteenth-century buildings.

Walter Charlton Hartridge, a native Savannahian and a graduate of Harvard University, modestly referred to himself as a historical researcher. His legacy to Savannah, however, will endure. He cared passionately about every building, street, square, and cobblestone in downtown Savannah, and long before there was any significant, well-organized preservation movement in Savannah, Walter Hartridge's efforts in the field of historic preservation constituted a one-man movement. Had it not been for his influence on the seven women who founded Historic Savannah Foundation, the thrust to modernize at the expense of irreplaceable architectural treasures might have prevailed.

As president of the Georgia Historical Society, 1952–62, Walter Hartridge spoke and wrote eloquently to promote the preservation of Savannah's historically and architecturally important buildings. He worked tirelessly and was instrumental in persuading individuals to save the Pink House, the Pirates' House, the Green-Meldrim House and the Davenport House, to mention just a few. He served with distinction as chair of the Savannah–Chatham County Historic Sites and Monuments Commission from 1967 until his death in 1974.

Historic Savannah Foundation's tribute to Hartridge after his death captured the heart and spirit with which he fought to enlighten and educate Savannah's citizens: "His scholarship formed an early and continuing ingredient of the historic preservation movement in Savannah. He loved this city without reservation and worked tirelessly and unselfishly his entire life to preserve its historic character. His legacy is vast; his ability to bring Savannah's history alive is legendary and his life will be an inspiration to the cause of historic preservation for years to come."

Anna Colquitt Hunter, artist and newspaper writer, the leader of the founding group, was cheered on by Walter Hartridge as she gathered the following co-founders after the destruction of the market: Elinor Grunsfeld Adler, Katharine Judkins Clark, Lucy Barrow McIntire, Dorothy Ripley Roebling, Nola Roos and Jane Adair Wright. Walter Hartridge was the chief advisor and mentor of the founders of Historic Savannah Foundation. If business leaders would not listen to a man whom they considered impractical, idealistic and visionary, they would listen to wives who were founders and completely convinced of his wisdom.

The new alliance held its organizational meeting on June 28, 1955, in the Gold Room of the old DeSoto Hotel with Anna Colquitt Hunter, chairwoman, presiding. At this meeting, Mrs. Hunter said: "It is because of periodic panics when landmarks are threatened that our group first initiated the idea of Historic Savannah. We believed that if an organization could be formed on a sound basis...[to] inaugurate a long range program, the danger of constant crises would be avoided." It was announced during the meeting that the Isaiah Davenport House (1821) at 324 East State Street was to be demolished and replaced by a parking lot for an adjacent funeral home. There was consensus among those present that the building should be saved. Hansell Hillyer reported that the owner, Mrs. E. L. Summerlin, was asking $22,000.

Soon after this meeting, Savannah native and former city alderman Jack Rauers was elected president of Historic Savannah, and a drive to raise $40,000 was initiated. The owner had reduced the asking price of the Davenport House to $18,000. Purchase of the house was made possible by a loan of $15,000 from Walter Hartridge and $3,000 raised by Freeman Jelks from Mrs. Raymond Demere, Mrs. Robert Groves, and Mrs. George Mercer. The house was ceded to Forward Savannah, a local nonprofit entity. Because the new preservation organization wanted to save historic buildings but did not want to own property, Family Service of Savannah moved its offices to the ground floor.

An article in the *Savannah Morning News* on November 9, 1955, covers a general membership meeting in the ballroom of the DeSoto Hotel. Jack Rauers announced that the organization had received its charter as a nonprofit entity dedicated to developing a long-range plan for preservation and restoration and that the Davenport House had been saved. Two years later, the fledgling preservation organization secured the Lachlan McIntosh House (1770) on East Oglethorpe Avenue and the Francis Stone House (1830) on

East State Street across from the Davenport House. In a talk in 1958 sponsored by the Gilmer Lecture Fund, Dr. Carl Feiss, a fellow of the American Institute of Architects and a trustee of the National Trust for Historic Preservation, recommended a professional inventory of property in the old city. Following his lecture, the Junior League of Savannah contributed $3,000 to Historic Savannah Foundation to fund his consulting services. The leadership of Historic Savannah Foundation recognized the importance of this recommendation because at this time, although the Historic American Buildings Survey had recorded a substantial number of buildings in Savannah in 1934, there was no general knowledge of Savannah's inventory of historically and architecturally valuable buildings—and, to date, no general awareness of the importance of saving the city's architectural patrimony.

To assist in saving historic properties in the late 1950s, Historic Savannah Foundation appealed to Mayor Malcolm Maclean for notification of impending demolition permits and a waiting period before such permits were granted. The result was a flexible seven-day stay of demolition by the City of Savannah to allow the Foundation's leaders to recruit individuals to find the money required to save an important building. At this time Historic Savannah Foundation was operating on a crisis-to-crisis basis, putting out fires—the loss of buildings all over the downtown area. We remember a cartoon in the *New Yorker* magazine which seemed to describe Savannah's plight. It was a Helen Hokinson sketch of her typically well-corseted matrons. One was saying to the other, "They are tearing down Boston and putting up something else."

During the presidency of Albert Stoddard in 1959, a row of four Savannah grey brick houses called Marshall Row (1854), at 230–244 East Oglethorpe Avenue, was saved dramatically at the eleventh hour. This rescue marked the beginning of Historic Savannah Foundation's aggressive real estate program to save the old city by buying an endangered building to save it from demolition and holding it for purchase by a buyer who would restore it. Lee's long career in historic preservation also really began with the saving of Marshall Row, which launched Historic Savannah Foundation's successful approach.

Some background information on Savannah grey bricks is important. Because of two great fires of the late eighteenth and early nineteenth centuries, the city government required buildings to be built of brick. An ingredient of the preferred brick was Savannah River sand. These bricks, called Savannah greys, had been kilned at the McAlpin Brickyard at the Hermitage Plantation, the destruction of which has been discussed in the Introduction. Savannah grey bricks were much in demand by the builders and buyers of tract housing under construction in the suburbs.

The Savannah grey brick used in the city's old housing was soft and porous and often covered by stucco or a nonporous decorative brick. Since this beautiful old brick was in such demand for suburban buildings, its price increased to three times the price of a common brick manufactured in the brickyards of the post-World War II period. This fact put enormous pressure on the old buildings in downtown Savannah. A demolition company could buy deteriorating unwanted buildings constructed of Savannah greys and make a 50 percent profit on the brick alone while retaining the property for a parking lot after the demolition. Parking lots were in demand because most merchants blamed declining sales on lack of parking rather than the growing strip shopping centers and gradual development of shopping malls in the ever-increasing suburban sprawl. A wrecker had bought the valuable Savannah grey bricks of the Marshall Row houses, which he could sell at a handsome profit to be reused in the construction of ranch-style suburban houses.

When it was revealed in the *Savannah Morning News* that Marshall Row, with its exquisite proportions, marble stairways, and handsome iron railings, was to be torn down, Historic Savannah Foundation launched a successful effort to save these important buildings. First of all, the threat of demolition to Marshall Row was imminent. The person who owned the property had sold the bricks for $6,000 to a wrecker who had begun demolition by tearing down the carriage houses at the rear of each building. Windows and doors had been removed from the main houses, and small fires built by vagrants had produced some holes in the beautiful pine floors. However, the buildings retained their architectural integrity, and to look out of the paneless windows across the boulevard to the Colonial Park and beyond to the soaring spires of the Cathedral of St. John the Baptist was an inspiring sight.

After discussion with Albert Stoddard, president of Historic Savannah, Lee immediately contacted the owner of the property, who explained that although he had sold the bricks for $6,000 to the wrecker, he still owned the land. He agreed to sell the underlying land for $45,000, but would not sell it to Historic Savannah Foundation. He said he might have to sue if the purchase was not completed, and he did not want involvement with a nonprofit civic organization. The demolition company was also contacted and asked to stop further demolition so that the organization could buy the bricks back from the wrecker. The first conversation concerned the price of the bricks. The wrecker asked $9,000, although he had paid only $6,000, including the bricks in the carriage houses which had already been sold.

A meeting of the Board of Trustees of Historic Savannah Foundation produced an agreement that the Foundation would pay the interest on a loan of $9,000 for the bricks still standing and $45,000 for the land. Lee found three other individuals who, acting with him for Historic Savannah Foundation, co-signed notes in the amount of the $54,000 needed to purchase the land and buildings. The others were Albert Stoddard, president of Historic Savannah, Karl Roebling, and Dr. Harry Duncan. The mechanics of this transaction were the result of desperation. Fortunately, the buildings were sold within a year to other persons who restored them, and the Foundation's project was a success. But had the project proved a failure, the bricks could have been sold for $6,000 and the land for at least $25,000. The location of Marshall Row, in the heart of the city near the main fire station, police headquarters, the county courthouse, and the commercial heart of the city, was excellent. The $23,000 loss which Historic Savannah Foundation might have incurred, spread out over eight hundred members, would not have been a burden—less than $30 per member, or about $6 per member spread out over five years.

This method of looking at the rescue of undervalued buildings was the key to the saving by Historic Savannah Foundation of threatened, yet valuable, buildings. The Foundation developed a method of operation based on the purchase of a threatened building to be held for resale to someone who would restore it. In this way, Historic Savannah Foundation became a conduit between the owner, who did not value his property, and the buyer, who would restore the historic building for contemporary use.

The *Savannah Morning News* gave prominent coverage to this event, recording Albert Stoddard's statement that the Foundation intended to "put the buildings into the hands of people who will restore them...profit is not the aim of the investment." By proving that it would not tolerate further senseless destruction of the city's irreplaceable heritage, the new preservation organization was beginning to have an impact.

When the first of the Marshall Row buildings was restored, Historic Savannah Foundation contacted the newspaper and had a reporter and editor look at the restored historic building next to three unrestored ones. The contrast was so great that the newspaper featured the restoration in its Sunday magazine supplement and claimed it a "miracle." Historic Savannah Foundation obtained permission from the new owner to open the building to the public on that Sunday. To everyone's amazement, hundreds came to see this "miracle," thus demonstrating dramatically the beauty and value of these graceful historic houses. This restoration showed clearly that downtown historic houses constituted an overlooked and underpriced resource. Increasing numbers of people began to take an interest in the rescue of the old buildings. Through the efforts of Anna Hunter, Hy Sobilof, an executive at H. W. Sloane Co., New York, was the first to purchase a Marshall Row house for restoration and use by his friend Conrad Aiken, the acclaimed poet. His birthplace next door was unavailable.

Having saved Marshall Row, Historic Savannah Foundation soon faced another challenge. Behind Marshall Row a fine, free-standing brick mansion at 205 East York Street was endangered. A businessman had purchased this outstanding four-story building with the hope of making it into offices. Claiming the cost was too high, he threatened to demolish the building and put a one-story concrete-block structure on the site. When Historic Savannah Foundation protested, he asked if it would buy the building, quoting a price of $21,000. The Foundation was finally able to purchase the building for $18,000, after the owner threatened demolition. About a month after the purchase, Lee realized that there was no "For Sale" sign on the building. Only forty-eight hours after a sign was installed, David Morrison, a prominent real estate agent, purchased the building and restored it as his offices. This transaction brought to the Foundation's attention the fact that its property acquisitions needed professional direction. Later, Historic Savannah Foundation asked Morrison to help coordinate its real estate initiatives, providing equitable fees to other agents.

Historic Savannah Foundation, with its determined and aggressive attitude, worked on buildings that were in immediate need of saving, and for the first time in many, many years, the old part of the city began to revive. It is hard to realize today that in the early 1960s downtown Savannah was almost completely dead as a residential area. One could buy magnificent historic buildings for very little, for there was hardly any interest in them.

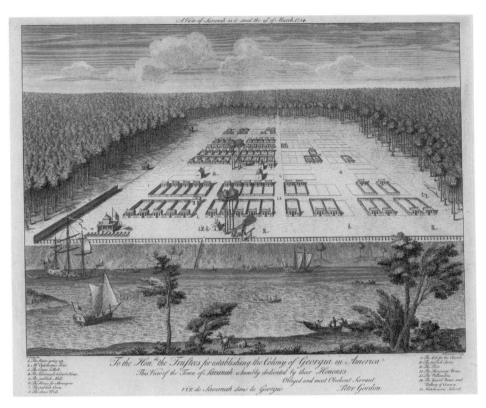

Oglethorpe-Gordon-Fourdrinier View of Savannah, 1734. Oglethorpe's concept of a town based upon a series of squares can be seen in Savannah today.

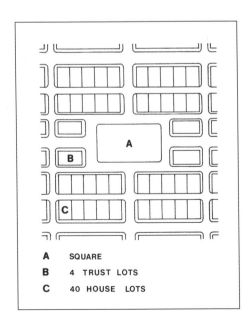

A SQUARE

B 4 TRUST LOTS

C 40 HOUSE LOTS

Savannah's city plan is basically an ancient grid that came from Greece, to Rome, to the British Isles, and then to this country. Its genius lies in its regularly recurring squares, orderly arrangements of house lots with carriage houses and lanes behind them, and rectangular street patterns.

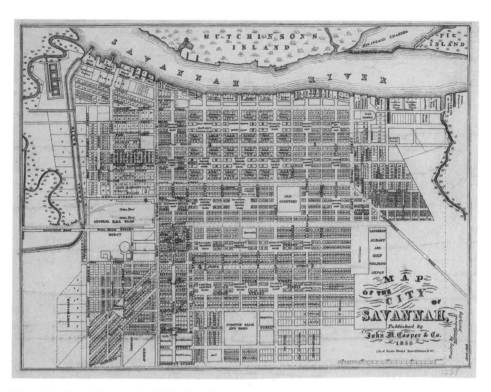

Map of the City of Savannah published by John M. Cooper & Co., 1856.

Walter Charlton Hartridge, a native Savannahian and a graduate of Harvard University, modestly referred to himself as a historical researcher. His legacy to Savannah, however, will endure. He cared passionately about every building, street, square, and cobblestone in downtown Savannah, and long before there was any significant, well-organized preservation movement in Savannah, Walter Hartridge's efforts in the field of historic preservation constituted a one-man movement.

Founders, Historic Savannah Foundation. Front, from left: Lucy Barrow McIntire, Elinor Grunsfeld Adler, Anna Colquitt Hunter. Back, from left: Nola McEvoy Roos, Jane Adair Wright, Katharine Judkins Clark. Not pictured: Dorothy Ripley Roebling

Lee Adler (left), president of Historic Savannah Foundation, presented a copy of Historic Savannah, *the Foundation's just-published inventory of historic buildings, to Albert H. Stoddard, immediate past president, in 1968.*

The Pink House was rescued by Alida Harper Fowlkes in the 1940s and converted to a tea room.

The Juliette Gordon Low Birthplace, a national Program Center for Girl Scouts, was purchased by the Girl Scouts' National Board in 1953. The building is on the northeast corner of Oglethorpe Avenue and Bull Street.

H. Hansell Hillyer, president of The Savannah
Gas Company, was Historic Savannah
Foundation's third president. He was the first
recipient of the Foundation's Davenport Trophy.

Reuben Grove Clark served as a vital member
of Historic Savannah Foundation's Steering
Committee from the mid-1950s through the
mid-1960s.

J. Frederick Waring (1902-1972) was active
in the preservation movement, and served as
chairman of the Save the Bay committee.

Anna Colquitt Hunter, who called together six
friends to establish Historic Savannah
Foundation in 1955.

The City Market, the work of Martin P. Muller and Augustus Schwaab, commanded Ellis Square from the early 1870s until it was demolished in 1954 to allow the construction of a parking garage. Its loss created the determination to stop further destruction of irreplaceable buildings.

This parking garage replaced the City Market.

The DeSoto Hotel was designed by William Gibbons Preston. One of Savannah's grandest buildings, it was completed in 1890. It was demolished despite objections from Historic Savannah Foundation in 1966.

The DeSoto Hilton opened in 1968.

Leopold Adler Co., known as Adler's, was Savannah's leading department store from the late nine-teenth century through the 1950s.

The Altmeyer building, a mid-nineteenth-century structure and home of Adler's department store, burned in the late 1950s. This building, which replaced it, has been improved in recent years.

HISTORIC SAVANNAH FOUNDATION'S CRITICAL YEARS: THE RISE TO NATIONAL PROMINENCE

The years 1958–68 saw the meteoric rise of Savannah's preservation movement to national prominence. In 1961, Lee succeeded Albert Stoddard, a native Savannahian with enduring personal commitment to historic preservation, as president of Historic Savannah Foundation. Lee was working at the local investment banking firm Varnedoe-Chisholm Inc. when he was elected at the Foundation's sixth annual meeting, open to the public and held at the Telfair Academy.

That meeting received extensive media coverage for the emphasis placed on the economic benefits of historic preservation through the development of tourism. A slide lecture, developed with assistance from the *Savannah Morning News,* showed that Knoxville, Tennessee, with a population of 132,000, was operating an annual $50 million tourist business as the gateway to the Smoky Mountains. Plans to establish a tourist and convention bureau in the Chamber of Commerce in Savannah were unveiled during this meeting. [Lee was awarded the Chamber's Order of the Gryphon Award in 1962 for his work in establishing this bureau, because he believed that the preservation movement would gain community-wide support if it was seen as a potential economic asset through the development of tourism.]

Historic Savannah Foundation moved its offices during 1961 from West Hull Street in a small ground-level apartment donated by Alida Harper Fowlkes to the ground floor of the Davenport House, and Ethelyn Nightingale McKinnon agreed to join its board to head the committee responsible for the development of the house as a museum. Emmeline King Cooper and then Nancy Nichols Calhoun had been employed as part-time secretaries during the Foundation's early years. Lucy Pope Cullen became the Foundation's first full-time executive secretary. Mrs. Cullen worked diligently with the organization's growing volunteer committees. Soon young Elizabeth Lattimore, native Savannahian and recent graduate of the University of Pennsylvania with a degree in the history of architecture, became Historic Savannah Foundation's star volunteer. Beth, who later married John Reiter, a local architect, was employed in 1968 by Historic Savannah Foundation, where she worked until 1974, leaving as associate director.

With a professional staff and the Davenport House as headquarters, Historic Savannah Foundation had a truly visible presence. Using many of her own resources, Ethelyn McKinnon supervised the restoration, decoration and furnishing of the Davenport House and, when the time came, recruited volunteer assistance to cope with an increasing number of visitors. The Juliette Gordon Low Birthplace, under the direction of Robertine McLendon, who was also a trustee of the Foundation, agreed to send all visiting Girl Scout troops through the Davenport House for twenty-five cents admission. This move proved to be extremely helpful during the Davenport House's early years as a museum. Ethelyn McKinnon's commitment and contributions to the Davenport House endured throughout her life.

After his election as president of Historic Savannah Foundation, Lee formed a steering committee and an executive committee from his board of directors. The steering committee met at least once a week, and the executive committee, which included the steering committee as well as board members who were chairing standing committees, met once a month. The entire board held quarterly meetings. Key members of the steering committee were Reuben Clark, president of the Savannah Bank; Hansell Hillyer, president of the Savannah Gas Company; and Albert Stoddard, trust officer at the Savannah Bank and past president of the organization. These men, along with Lucy Barrow McIntire, a founder, Muriel Barrow Bell and Robertine McLendon, met regularly with Lee to develop methods and techniques to finance the acquisition of threatened valuable historic places and to plan the day-to-day activities of the Foundation.

Preservation efforts in Charleston became a model for Historic Savannah Foundation. Historic Charleston Foundation, which had enormous influence, had conducted and published in 1944 an inventory of the city's historic and architecturally valuable buildings. The publication, *This is Charleston*, enabled citizens and all who knew and visited Charleston to see which buildings were valuable. Ansonborough, one of the outer parts of old Charleston, was deteriorating, and Historic Charleston Foundation was involved actively in reclaiming rundown and neglected structures in the area. Historic Charleston Foundation, a nonmember, nonprofit organization, had raised money for a revolving fund to purchase, restore and re-sell important buildings. The organization was engaged in restoration work, an approach not taken by Historic Savannah Foundation. Because Charleston's preservation organization had been operating much longer than Savannah's and was protected by a municipal ordinance, it was able to gather funds for restoration without enormous pressure to save hundreds of threatened buildings. Although the problems facing these two beautiful neighboring cities differed, the techniques used by Historic Charleston Foundation proved valuable to Savannah. Historic Charleston, with assistance from Frances Edmunds, its expert director, was extremely helpful to Historic Savannah Foundation, which even went so far as to appropriate Charleston's slogan, "Historic preservation goes hand in hand with economic progress," as well as its methods of acquiring endangered properties to hold for resale to individuals who would restore them.

Historic Savannah Foundation's first brochure, designed by Ray Dilley, a newspaper reporter and editor of the Pigeonhole Press, was published in 1962. At this time, the fee for regular annual membership was $5 per person because the leadership wanted to reach the widest public across all segments of the population. Membership numbered approximately eight hundred. The brochure announced that the Foundation was staffed professionally, had head-quarters in the Davenport House, and was affiliated with the National Trust for Historic Preservation. Goals included increased public awareness of the importance of historic preservation in Savannah, an increased tourist indus-try, preservation legislation for the downtown area, and accessible and ade-quate funding for the purchase and improvement of downtown property.

Historic Savannah Foundation worked to maintain diverse uses of proper-ty in the downtown area. In the early 1960s, the Savannah Electric Company considered moving to the south side, but was persuaded by Historic Savannah Foundation to build its new building on the east end of River Street. In 1964, Historic Savannah Foundation worked with the city to improve lighting, side-walks and surfacing on River Street and to retain the old-fashioned quality by using Belgian block as paving material rather than asphalt.

Private individuals who were encouraged by Historic Savannah Foundation's activities made significant contributions to the restoration of the city. Alida Harper Fowlkes continued her projects, restoring more than ten buildings in the Madison Square–Orleans Square–Jones Street area. Mrs. Fowlkes bequeathed her house, the historic McAlpin House, designed by Charles Cluskey, to the Society of the Cincinnati for its state headquarters. Stella Henderson refurbished over twenty buildings in the Green Square and Warren Square areas. Georgia Fawcett was also a restorer of note. The family of Henry Dunn did substantial restoration work on West Gaston Street. James A. Williams restored buildings in Washington Ward. Mills Lane, Jr. engaged in significant restoration in the St. Julian Street and Price Street neighbor-hoods and contributed funds for the improvement of several squares. Mr. Lane moved the Mongin House (1797) to the southeast trust lot on Warren Square, where it was purchased and restored by Mr. and Mrs. John W. Carswell.

Although the Girl Scouts of America had purchased the birthplace of Juliette Gordon Low on the northeast corner of Oglethorpe Avenue at Bull Street in 1951 for use as a national center, the other buildings along Oglethorpe Avenue between Bull and Drayton Streets were in danger of dem-olition. Historic Savannah Foundation purchased 18 East Oglethorpe Avenue for $54,000 in 1963 to assist with the stabilization of this important block, rescuing the building after the roof had been torn off in the demolition process. After holding the building for two years, the Foundation sold the property to David Meddin, realtor, who restored it for his office.

In 1967, 15 West Perry Street was to be torn down for a parking lot. The house had been left to heirs, but only one cared about it. May Bond Screven Rhodes allowed Historic Savannah to purchase her undivided interest, and although the owner of the remaining undivided interest offered the Foundation $5,000 more than it paid Mrs. Rhodes, the Foundation refused to comply and allow demolition. After acquiring full title to her property and holding it for nearly five years, the Foundation sold it to Dr. and Mrs. Edward Downing, who restored this beautiful house for their residence. The Downings became major investors in downtown property and champions of historic preservation.

Following Carl Feiss's recommendation made during his Gilmer Lecture in 1958, Prof. Paul Dulaney and Prof. Frederick Nichols with their team from the University of Virginia conducted a professional inventory in 1962. They studied approximately two thousand buildings in downtown Savannah, and of these, eleven hundred were recognized as having architectural and/or historical significance. One of Historic Savannah's priorities became to have this inventory published to provide the public with important knowledge regarding the historical and architectural value of buildings in the old city. Such a publication would be an important resource for evaluating Savannah's historic real estate.

To further the goal of increasing the public's awareness of the importance of historic preservation, Lee and his steering committee recommended a study of Savannah's potential for tourism. This committee was keenly aware of the need to interpret the value of historic preservation to the business and governmental sectors of the community and knew that in the eyes of most people, at that time, an old building was considered less valuable than a new one. Preservation for historic or aesthetic reasons was not accepted. Preservation for economic benefit, on the other hand, might be considered desirable.

Historic Savannah Foundation brought Thomas G. McCaskey, Vice President and Director of Development of Colonial Williamsburg, to Savannah in 1962 to address the Foundation's trustees and the senior group of Leadership Savannah, an organization of young business leaders. His opinions would have a tremendous influence on Savannah's preservation movement and on the growth of the city's tourist industry. Mr. McCaskey's words, printed in prominent news stories, projected a rosy future for tourism: "Savannah has a great tourist potential in its fine buildings surrounding green squares in a downtown area bounded by a unique riverfront and Factors' Walk complex. These assets must be protected so that this city of amazing beauty can fulfill its promise in the travel world. Destroy that beauty and you destroy an asset that is unmatched anywhere in this country."

After Mr. McCaskey's visit in 1962, Historic Savannah Foundation continued to work with him and with the Chamber of Commerce to develop plans for an expanded report on Savannah's potential for tourism. Colonial Williamsburg made a generous contribution to Savannah's future by allowing Mr. McCaskey to work in Savannah at no cost other than his expenses, which Historic Savannah Foundation underwrote. His comprehensive plan, *Savannah, Georgia, as a Travel Destination,* was published by Historic Savannah Foundation and the Savannah Area Chamber of Commerce in 1965. This report includes an analysis of the number and condition of sites to be visited by tourists, visitor accommodations, restaurants, parking and transportation, building an image, developing specific tours, maps, brochures, highway signs, coordination of printed materials, advertising, promotional tools, guide books, publicity, special events, training of local people, creating the right community attitude, and more. The McCaskey report proved to have inestimable value to the development of Savannah's tourist industry, which was earning less than $100,000 in the 1950s and which today is one of the city's top four industries, bringing in annual revenues of $1 billion. By this time, Savannah's general public was beginning to recognize that visitors would come from near and far and would pay to enjoy the city's historic buildings, museums and old-world atmosphere.

The annual celebration of the founding of Savannah in 1733 was inaugurated in 1965 as an additional tool to increase public awareness of Savannah's historic and architectural heritage. Robertine McLendon first suggested recognition of the founding of the Georgia colony in relation to Savannah's preservation movement. She understood the public education value of a community-wide annual celebration. Robbie McLendon called Emma (then chair of public relations for Historic Savannah Foundation) and asked that the *Savannah Morning News* be contacted about a banner headline on February 12, the day of General Oglethorpe's landing here to establish the Georgia colony. Emma's conversation with Frank Rossiter, city editor, convinced her that in order to get any coverage, a newsworthy event must be created. Thus began the annual Georgia Day celebration.

When Judge Alexander A. Lawrence, speaker at the first annual Georgia Day celebration in 1965, predicted that the event could become the biggest day on Savannah's calendar, he probably had no idea of the degree to which his prophesy would be realized. S. Joseph Ward, Jr., assistant to the director of the Chamber of Commerce, chaired the first Georgia Day. Activity began with the laying of a wreath on the spot where General Oglethorpe pitched his tent on February 12, 1733, as he established the thirteenth English colony in America. The main program took place in Washington Square, which had been landscaped recently through the efforts of Mills B. Lane, Jr., president of the Citizens and Southern National Bank, who then lived in Atlanta. (The bank had been founded by his father in Savannah.) Lee, as president of Historic Savannah Foundation, was master of ceremonies. Highlights included a welcome from Mayor Malcolm Maclean, who read a proclamation by Georgia Governor Carl Sanders. Norris Pindar III, taking the part of General Oglethorpe, gave a dramatic reading of one of the founder's reports to the Trustees of the colony. Mike Murrin, a Boy Scout, was dignified in the role of Chief Tomochichi. Students from Bartlett Junior High School sang songs of the colonial period, and the Savannah High School band played "God Save the Queen." An editorial in the *Savannah Morning News*, February 13, 1965, expressed the hope that the celebration, hailed as a success, would become a major tourist attraction.

In subsequent years, Historic Savannah Foundation added a luncheon to the expanding events and used the occasion to tell the community about its accomplishments and to involve the general public in support of its goals. Nationally prominent figures have been attracted as speakers for the Georgia Day Luncheon. Among them in the early years were Georgia governors Lester Maddox and Jimmy Carter; Dr. Alexander Heard, chancellor of Vanderbilt University; Walter Hickel, secretary of the Department of the Interior; William Ruckelshaus, secretary of the Department of the Interior; United States Congresswoman Lindy Boggs; and Michael Egan, of the Justice Department.

The Davenport Trophy was established in 1965 and so named because Historic Savannah Foundation recognized the symbolism of its first dramatic rescue from the wrecker's ball—the house which had become its headquarters as well as one of the city's outstanding museums. The first Davenport Trophy was presented to Hansell Hillyer, past president of the Foundation, emphasizing the fact that "the trophy is given only when outstanding service merits it, not necessarily on an annual basis....The first recipient is a person whose sustained effort has meant monumental achievement for Historic Savannah Foundation." The citation on the certificate that accompanied an engraved Revere bowl of sterling silver stated: "As a past president, he has participated in significant area restoration, serving on the Board, Executive and Steering Committees, always contributing in large measure. The culmination of his effort came in 1964 when his genius devised the plan to raise the much-needed money for the Revolving Redevelopment Fund. His interest in the historic part of our city extends over a 20-year period."

By the early 1960s, the broad scope and sheer volume of activity made it necessary for the Foundation to hire an executive director. Volunteers alone could no longer cope with the huge task of saving Savannah's architectural heritage. Emma was president of the Junior League of Savannah from 1965 to 1967 and had been on Historic Savannah Foundation's executive committee as chair of public relations since 1959. She assisted in tailoring a major project for the Junior League because she was in a position to know the needs of the two organizations.

A project undertaken by the Junior League requires a financial contribution as well as administrative and volunteer service. The Foundation's proposal, accepted by the Junior League, asked that the League pay $7,500 a year for two years towards the salary of an executive director and that it contribute $5,000 a year for two years toward the publication of the Foundation's inventory of buildings worthy of preservation. The proposal further specified that two League members should serve on Historic Savannah Foundation's steering committee (a committee of officers) and that five League members should serve on its executive committee, which was composed of the officers and chairs of standing committees.

Thus two League members were chosen to be officers of the Foundation and five to head committees that could develop definite programs and put a great many volunteers to work. The League chairs serving on Historic Savannah's executive committee really acted as para-professionals, performing jobs necessary to the Foundation for which no money was available to hire professional staff. The five committees were Georgia Day, volunteers, tours, program, and public relations. This project so thoroughly involved the League membership and afforded such satisfactory placement, utilizing a great diversity of talents and interests, that in 1968 the League voted an additional $7,500 to extend the project for a third year.

With the approval of the steering and executive committees, Lee sought advice from the National Trust regarding the hiring of an executive director. He was told to consider directors of Chambers of Commerce or high school principals. And so it was that Reid Williamson, a graduate of Yale, then married to Kitty Glendinning of Savannah, was persuaded to return from Atlanta, where he was employed by the Chamber of Commerce, to fill the position of executive director of Historic Savannah Foundation. The year was 1965. Reid Williamson came to direct a well-organized foundation staffed with only an executive secretary. Responsible volunteer committees were doing the critical work of fund-raising, saving threatened historic properties throughout the downtown area, and educating the public about the economic and aesthetic value of historic preservation.

A list of properties purchased for resale to individuals who would restore them shows the need for professional direction and the extent of real estate activity in which Historic Savannah Foundation was involved from 1962 to 1968: Armstrong College properties; Troup Trust properties; the Oliver Sturges House; the courthouse annex designed by Charles Cluskey on the southwest trust lot of Oglethorpe Square; the Hamilton-Turner House on Lafayette Square; the 101 West Congress Street commercial redevelopment project; and the Pulaski Square/West Jones Street residential redevelopment project.

Historic Savannah Foundation had conducted a successful capital funds campaign in 1964 to establish a revolving fund which would finance its real estate transactions. A foundation called Forward Savannah, precursor to the Savannah Foundation, contributed $75,000 as a challenge grant to be matched by Historic Savannah Foundation, enabling it to launch a drive that would raise more than $200,000. Hansell Hillyer, president of the Savannah Gas Company, gave critical assistance with this first significant capital funds campaign by creating a list of forty business leaders in Savannah and Atlanta who would be approached to contribute to a revolving fund. It evolved that Lee was chosen to meet with Mills Lane, Jr. at 6:30 a.m. at his Citizens and Southern Bank office in Atlanta with a manifesto on Savannah's preservation movement. The result of this meeting, a contribution in the amount of $50,000, signified this important banker's endorsement and his commitment to historic preservation. Savannah's emphasis, modeled on Charleston's similar fund for securing valuable properties for restoration, would be securing properties in order to place them in the hands of individuals who would restore them. Reuben Clark, president of the locally owned Savannah Bank and Trust Company, was successful in his commitment to secure financing for Historic Savannah Foundation's capital and administrative needs.

With a successful campaign behind it, Historic Savannah Foundation, using its still-unpublished professional inventory, targeted its first area restoration projects, a commercial redevelopment in the 100 West Congress Street block and a residential redevelopment in the Pulaski Square/West Jones Street area. The West Congress Street commercial project was patterned after the Norwich, England, Magdalen Street Project, sponsored by England's Civic Trust. A pilot project of Historic Savannah, the revitalization of this mercantile block included the Peeples–Stubbs twin buildings, threatened by demolition, and other fine three-story buildings of stucco over brick with cast iron ornamentation dating from the 1880s. Robert D. Gunn, architect and future president of Historic Savannah Foundation, designed a modern building, compatible in scale and materials, that was constructed as infill on a vacant lot in the block. The city installed new brick sidewalks, lighting, and landscaping.

The Pulaski Square/West Jones Street project was selected because of the quality of the buildings and the fact that this rental property had been vacated by railroad workers after the Central of Georgia Railroad closed its shops. Demolition for the coveted Savannah grey bricks was thus again prevented.

An article in the *Savannah Evening Press,* November 10, 1965, describes the Pulaski Square effort as "the largest redevelopment undertaking by Historic Savannah since its founding in 1954." The inventory showed more than one hundred valuable buildings in this area, which included two blocks on West Jones Street from Whitaker to Tattnall and the entire Pulaski Ward.

Following Historic Charleston's effort in the Ansonborough section of that city, Historic Savannah Foundation acquired options and delayed sales contracts on forty-five pieces of property. This was done with no publicity through real estate agents who shielded Historic Savannah Foundation's interest so that prices in these deteriorating neighborhoods would not escalate. With permission from the Savannah Bank, signs were made using the bank's attractive logo of the SS *Savannah*, the first steamship to sail from Savannah across the Atlantic Ocean. The area was opened to the public on a weekend. Many of Historic Savannah"s members and members of the Junior League of Savannah volunteered to show the buildings to persons who might be interested in buying and restoring them. The *Savannah Morning News* did a supplement with numerous photographs to explain the project. In spite of a soft housing market and a rise in interest rates, on the weekend of October 15, 1965, fourteen thousand people came to see the project, which had large signs at the end of the streets to proclaim Historic Savannah Foundation's Pulaski Square/West Jones Street redevelopment project.

The Foundation put only a small markup from its cost on the buildings, so that persons who bought buildings to restore would get them as reasonably as possible. The slight markups covered legal fees, taxes, insurance, and a small amount for administrative costs. A brochure identified the buildings in the area and explained their attributes.

By buying as many properties as possible in this important area, Historic Savannah Foundation created a security net so that buyers were assured that their neighbors were also going to restore. For a potential homeowner this took much of the risk out of being a lone and vulnerable urban pioneer. Historic Savannah Foundation began to see itself as an urban developer with the advantage of having all the necessary amenities in place: sidewalks, streets, gutters, trees, fire plugs, street lighting—and houses. The Foundation merely secured the area by acquiring properties that would have gone to a wrecker and transferring them to owners who would restore them to revitalize a run-down neighborhood.

One incident brought about improved techniques. Legal protective preservation covenants were attached to the deeds of all the properties Historic Savannah Foundation bought. Since there were no historic zoning laws in Savannah, these enforceable covenants assured that owners in successive generations would not alter the historic properties without the approval of Historic Savannah Foundation. Later, easements on properties not owned by Historic Savannah Foundation were applied to supplement the protection program. Covenants stated that no building could be demolished and that there could be no changes to the exterior without the permission of Historic Savannah Foundation. A person who bought property from the Foundation must offer it first to the Foundation if it was to be sold. One fine wooden building was bought and held for speculation. This distressing possibility was corrected after a telephone call to Frances Edmunds in Charleston produced this covenant: a purchaser of a property from Historic Savannah Foundation must begin restoration within six months and complete it within eighteen months.

On the opening day of the Pulaski Square/ West Jones Street project, November 21, 1965, Lee, in his fourth year as president of Historic Savannah Foundation, said: "Today is a landmark in the revitalization of downtown Savannah … for Historic Savannah Foundation has maintained, since its beginning eleven years ago, that restoration of the worthy buildings in the historic heart of our city is absolutely essential to the support of a first class Central Business District. Nineteen months ago, the Board of Trustees of Historic Savannah started to raise funds for a Revolving Redevelopment Fund for area restoration. Realizing that if houses of architectural and historical merit were bought in blighted areas, and acquired properly and one at a time, entire wards could be saved and consequently restored, Historic Savannah obtained a grant from Forward Savannah and then more than matched funds to operate the Foundation and begin two projects…first the 100 Block of West Congress Street…and second, this residential area development project that you will see today… As you will see, there is a surge of successful work afoot in downtown restoration. Historic Savannah has saved over forty-five buildings in the past few years."

In the early 1960s, Mayor Malcolm Maclean told Historic Savannah Foundation of Armstrong Junior College's plans to become a four-year college as part of the University of Georgia system. The college, then housed in six buildings in Monterey Ward, with its administration in the fine Italianate mansion designed by Henrik Wallin and built for $1 million for George

Armstrong in 1919, was planning to acquire property for expansion extending north on Bull Street. In the name of improvement, the college would demolish most of the existing buildings on Bull Street as far north as Liberty Street and replace them with new brick construction in the style of the Gamble building built by the college and located on the northeast trust lot of Monterey Square. (Ironically, this building is the *one* building singled out by Edmund Bacon in his book *Design of Cities* as an example of architecture which "fails to meet the demands of its site.") Also designated for the wrecker's ball by the college was Gordon Row, an outstanding block of mid-nineteenth-century houses extending along Gordon Street between Whitaker and Barnard Streets. This block was to be used for appropriate faculty housing.

"Revitalization" plans of this sort would have decimated the heart of Savannah, removing many of the city's finest buildings along its most prominent street. Every piece of property desired by the college had the highest rating in Historic Savannah's yet-to-be-published professional inventory. The leadership of Historic Savannah informed the regents of the University of Georgia of the Foundation's opposition to Armstrong's plans for expansion, proposing that the college expand in a southerly direction along Barnard Street just two blocks west of Bull Street. This was an area that needed revitalization, one that could tolerate new construction. Negotiations between Historic Savannah and the University of Georgia included visits by the regents to look at the properties under consideration by Armstrong. They little understood the value of the existing historic properties owned by Armstrong College, most of which were considered unsuitable by the university officials. The college was not interested in expanding along Barnard Street; it desired a contiguous campus in new buildings along Bull Street. But under pressure from Historic Savannah Foundation, expansion plans were suspended.

The issue was finally settled by Mills B. Lane, when he learned from Walter Hartridge that Lane's family house on the corner of Gaston and Drayton Streets in Savannah might be threatened. Mr. Lane made a gift to the college of land outside the city along the Abercorn Street extension. Historic Savannah Foundation then purchased the six downtown properties owned by the college in a lump-sum bid of $235,000. The transfer of property to the Foundation was completed March 1, 1967. Historic Savannah Foundation sold the properties for the exact purchase prices as follows: lot 39, Quattlebaum property northeast corner of Whitaker and Gaston, to Wayne Cunningham; lot 40, Lane property, 20 West Gaston, to Dr. Peter Scardino; lots 41, 42 and 43, including Jenkins Hall, an auditorium built by the college, and the Armstrong House, to James A. Williams; the Hunt Building, on the southwest corner of Bull and Gordon Streets, to the Savannah Art

Association; the Gamble Building on Monterey Square to the Savannah Foundation. Again, Historic Savannah Foundation had fulfilled its purpose to save important historic buildings and turn them over to individuals who would put them to contemporary use and maintain them responsibly, with no financial profit to itself.

The large trust lots, two on the east and two on the west side of each square, are Savannah's sites for monumental buildings. Here are found many of the city's finest churches, public buildings, and mansions. During the 1960s, Historic Savannah Foundation saved the following major properties on trust lots: the Italianate Mercer House on the southwest trust lot on Monterey Square, designed by John S. Norris and built c. 1860; the Oliver Sturges House, built in 1818 on Reynolds Square; the Cluskey buildings on Oglethorpe Square, dating from 1859; and the Hamilton-Turner House, 1873, on Lafayette Square.

The Citizens and Southern Bank intended to destroy the Sturges House, the remaining half of a double house that had been demolished in the 1930s, and to use the property for much-needed parking spaces. After finding suitable parking for the bank, Historic Savannah Foundation purchased this exceptional house of Philadelphia pressed brick for $76,000, a high price in those days. In order to finance it, trustees and friends of Historic Savannah put up unsecured funds allowing the Foundation to get a $50,000 loan at prime rate. Much of the $26,000 put up privately was interest-free and had no strings attached except possible repayment after the resale of the house to a person who would restore it. Historic Savannah Foundation paid interest on this property for seven years, and although the sale to Charles H. Morris was finally made at a loss, the building today is fully restored, again demonstrating the basic reason for Historic Savannah Foundation's existence: to assume the financial burden of showing the way to practical modern use of fine old buildings. The substantial interest charges, taxes, insurance premiums, and principal repayments did not stop the Foundation from acquiring irreplaceable historic properties, nor did the fact that Historic Savannah Foundation was often forced to buy at a premium and sell at a loss.

The handsome, four-story double residence of Savannah grey brick adorned with iron balconies designed by Charles Cluskey on Oglethorpe Square was slated for demolition to make room for a fourteen-story glass and concrete annex to the courthouse on Wright Square. The owner of the Cluskey building had planned to sell the Savannah greys at a handsome profit before offering the land to the county, but agreed to sell the building to Historic Savannah Foundation for $175,000, an exorbitant price at that time. To make the purchase possible, the owner agreed to amazingly lenient terms:

$1,000 down payment and $14,000 due at the end of six months. Interest payments would follow for eighteen months, and then $4,000 a month would be paid for the next eight years with a balloon note at the end. Fortunately, Historic Savannah Foundation was soon able to sell the building, for conversion into law offices, at a loss of $25,000. The Foundation considered the loss a contribution to the cultural heritage and urban vitality of Savannah.

The destruction of the Hamilton-Turner House on Lafayette Square, which had a high rating in the Foundation's inventory, would have constituted a significant loss to Savannah and to the buildings in this important and historic neighborhood. Saving this fine Victorian house—three stories over a basement, of stucco over brick with a mansard roof and a cupola with iron fleur-de-lys trim—illustrates one of the dramatic successes of Historic Savannah Foundation. Dating from 1873, the building was owned by the Catholic Diocese of Savannah as part of a concentration of properties near the Cathedral of St. John the Baptist on Abercorn Street. An out-of-scale elementary school constructed on the northeast trust lot in the 1940s needed parking and play spaces, and the diocese planned to demolish the Turner House for this purpose. After negotiations, Historic Savannah Foundation acquired a vacant lot on Macon Street east of Lincoln and persuaded the diocese to accept it as a site for the proposed playground/parking lot. The Foundation then purchased the Turner House, which it held until it found a buyer to restore it.

Troup Square, on Habersham Street between Harris and Charlton Streets, in the early 1960s was fenced with a chain-link fence and used as a playground by the Catholic Church schools. The Catholic diocese also owned Troup Trust, eight row houses at 412–424 East Macon Street and 324 Habersham Street. Built in 1876, they are noteworthy examples of row houses built soon after the Civil War. Each building is three stories of Savannah grey brick construction with sandstone window lintels and sills and a wood cornice with brackets over brick dentils. Cast-iron balconies decorate three of the buildings. Historic Savannah Foundation purchased these buildings and immediately advertised them for resale along with another empty row built in 1881 for John McDonough, 410–424 East Charlton Street. The houses on Charlton Street are three stories of Savannah grey brick overlaid with stucco. Cast-iron lintels and sills decorate the windows, and there is a wood cornice with brackets. Both rows were resold by Historic Savannah Foundation to owners who restored them as residences.

As all this was happening, Historic Savannah Foundation attracted the attention of Donald Naismith, an officer at the Savannah Housing Authority, who worked with the U.S. Department of Housing and Urban Development

(HUD). The housing authority, with Historic Savannah Foundation and the city, focused on one of the earliest plans to use an urban renewal conservation program. This project involved HUD 312 loans, which were designed to lend federal dollars for downtown restoration as well as for new buildings in the suburbs. These three percent loans offered at half the prime interest rate for twenty to thirty years could be taken as a second or third mortgage on the property. Successful meetings were called with residents and owners of properties in Troup Ward. Soon there was activity in these areas that had long been neglected. In addition to the property owners who were excited by the offer of funds for rehabilitation, many new people bought property here. Middle-income families became ardent historic preservationists.

As important buildings and areas were saved and downtown revitalization brought residents back to the National Historic District, citizens began to appreciate the special qualities of their city. In the preservation world, Savannah's triumph over bulldozers and urban renewal programs that gutted the hearts of so many cities in the 1960s was heralded as the success of the decade. Articles on Savannah's renaissance appeared in newspapers and magazines across the country. *Antiques* magazine published an issue on Savannah in 1966 with its cover featuring the Lafayette balcony at the Owens-Thomas House. Alice Winchester, editor, says of Savannah in her introduction: "Beautiful, thriving, historic, progressive, tranquil....in these terms and many others have visitors attempted to sum up the city's special character. Savannah is the oldest city in Georgia, but one of the youngest coastal towns. We present Antiques at Savannah, and devote the following pages to its historic architecture and early crafts, its preservation movement." Ms. Winchester gives special thanks to Henry D. Green of Madison, Georgia, "whose enthusiasm for this project was largely responsible for our undertaking it." Historic Savannah Foundation purchased twenty-five thousand reprints of the issue at $2.00 per copy and used them for years in its public relations and marketing program.

The year 1966 was busy and important for Historic Savannah Foundation. As a result of its inventory by architects from the University of Virginia of properties in downtown Savannah, the United States Department of the Interior designated this 2.2-square-mile area as the nation's largest urban national historic district. This was also the year when Historic Savannah Foundation purchased the William Scarbrough House, designed by William Jay in 1818 and one of the outstanding American mansions of its time. The house had functioned as a school for children of African descent from 1876 until 1966, when school integration laws forced it to close. Mrs. Craig Barrow gave her share to Historic Savannah Foundation, and the Foundation purchased the remaining shares from members of the family. The ambitious new Scarbrough Foundation was formed to raise money to restore the house, and the deed was turned over to this foundation by Historic Savannah Foundation.

After more than six years of work, the Foundation's inventory was published in 1968 in a volume entitled *Historic Savannah*, a publication made possible by the Junior League and the Wormsloe Foundation. Although Historic Savannah Foundation had been using the inventory to guide its preservation activities since 1962, now the information would be available to the public. A publication by Paul Muldawer entitled *Historic Preservation Plan*, which established criteria for new construction in the National Historic District, was funded by the Department of Housing and Urban Renewal during this year. Also in 1968, the state legislature passed enabling legislation for historic zoning in Savannah's historic district. Savannah's first historic zoning ordinance would be passed by a three-to-one vote in a public referendum in 1972.

Anna Hunter, a founder of Historic Savannah Foundation, spoke to the Friends of the Library, February 13, 1968. She summarized Historic Savannah Foundation's decade of achievement with the following tribute to Lee's leadership: "It is not often that a burgeoning civic project has the good fortune to have the man of the hour loom on the horizon at a critical hour. Since Lee took over the helm, fantastic progress has been made. He has served five terms [ten years]…in a critical and progressive time. It would be impossible to list all the accomplishments of Historic Savannah under Mr. Adler's leadership, and it has been a leadership in which he has been at the very vortex of the whirlpool that historic preservation has become. He has put Historic Savannah Foundation on a big business basis, driven relentlessly to bring the city to which he is dedicated to national recognition and has pursued every possible avenue of advancement open to the city in a day of booming urban improvement."

THE NATIONAL TRUST FOR HISTORIC
PRESERVATION: A NATIONAL AND LOCAL PRESENCE

Thanks to Historic Savannah Foundation's relationship with Carl Feiss, FAIA, who in 1958 had recommended the property inventory, Lee and the board of directors recognized the importance of affiliation with the National Trust for Historic Preservation. Chartered by the United States Congress as a nonprofit entity in 1949, the National Trust was engaged in the important effort to save the nation's architectural heritage and also provided professional assistance and access to other communities.

The National Trust had existed for only twelve years when we went to our first annual conference in New York in 1961. Lee has attended almost every annual meeting since then. He immediately understood the importance of affiliation with this prestigious national organization. He was its champion in Savannah and took full advantage of making contacts which would further the cause of preservation at home. From Charleston, Annapolis, and Pittsburgh he learned the various approaches to urban preservation and revitalization, and at his invitation, nationally acclaimed experts visited Savannah to evaluate the city plan, architectural treasures, and tourist potential.

In 1962, Nathaniel Owings, of Skidmore, Owings and Merrill, who had spoken at our first National Trust meeting, accepted an invitation to speak in Savannah, beginning Historic Savannah Foundation's practice of bringing to the city nationally recognized experts in the field of architecture and historic preservation. We shall always remember his awed response to Chippewah Square with Daniel Chester French's monument to James Oglethorpe. We knew the critical importance of getting the preservation message to the entire community, and we believed that it would be helpful if Savannahians could know about preservation efforts in other cities. Helen Bullock, who published the National Trust's newsletter, agreed to send a series of feature stories highlighting preservation successes in cities along the eastern seaboard. The *Savannah Morning News* published this series on its editorial page, helping to increase local awareness of preservation efforts on a national level.

After successfully launching Historic Savannah Foundation's revolving fund in 1964, Lee visited the Lila Wallace–Reader's Digest Fund in New York in an effort to obtain a substantial grant for Savannah's fund. When he learned that this foundation would give only to a national organization, he encouraged the Wallace Foundation to contribute to the National Trust for Historic Preservation. Thus the Trust established a revolving fund with its first grant from the Wallace Foundation in 1966.

We had been particularly impressed by the 1966 National Trust meeting in Philadelphia when Charles Woodward was chair. Headquarters were at the Bellevue Stratford Hotel, and the fact that hotel employees were on strike created an unusual atmosphere. Mr. Woodward was an omnipresent chair, deeply concerned about the comfort and well-being of each person. But all those attending cooperated to make up for the lack of service at the hotel, and a cheerful atmosphere prevailed with little or no complaint. The excellent meeting featured a panel of experts telling about Philadelphia's recent accomplishments in the field of urban renewal, restoration and redevelopment. Edmund Bacon, who had spearheaded the Society Hill revitalization, was a member of this panel, which was held at the Academy of Music. [An unusual event occurred during a luncheon held at Head House Square. The Society Hill Restoration and Renewal Project had just been completed and was being featured. Edmund Bacon, who had directed the project, had spoken at the opening panel. But there were those who regretted the loss of even one historic building, and the eminent Charles Peterson was one of these. As we were enjoying our lunch, we heard a funeral dirge. A parade of preservationists wearing mourning bands passed by bearing aloft an effigy of Ed Bacon!]

The National Preservation Act of 1966 had become public law by act of the Eighty-ninth Congress just before the Philadelphia meeting. The act authorized the Secretary of the Interior "to establish a program of making grants-in-aid to the states…as well as to the National Trust for Historic Preservation, chartered by Act of Congress, approved October 26, 1949." The optimistic and dedicated delegate body which heard the report, "Decade of Decision," given by Gordon Gray, chairman of the board, understood that the preservation movement was entering a period of growth, accomplishment, and national recognition. We grasped the implications of Gray's report and optimistically resolved to interpret at home the growing national recognition of the importance of historic preservation.

A delegation from Historic Savannah Foundation attended the 1967 annual meeting of the National Trust for Historic Preservation held in St. Louis, Missouri. Reid Willliamson, HSF's executive director, had arrived at the meeting a day early and had invited the Trust to meet in Savannah at a future date. This would be the first annual conference of the National Trust in our city. When we arrived in St. Louis, there was a message from Reid saying that Savannah would host the National Trust's annual meeting in 1970. This was not to be, however, for we soon learned that 1970 would be the year of Charleston's three-hundredth anniversary. The trust would have to meet in Charleston that year. Savannah was offered a choice of 1968 or 1972. The delegation chose 1968, leaving just one year to prepare for the meeting.

When we met with the planning committee to begin work on the meeting in Savannah, we realized how much it had meant to be given an overview of the current status of historic preservation in Philadelphia at the outset of the meeting there. We made sure that the format of the National Trust meeting in Savannah would include an opening program which would outline the goals and accomplishments of Historic Savannah Foundation to set the tone for those attending the meeting. This idea became "The Savannah Story," presented by a panel which included Robert D. Gunn, president; Walter Hartridge II, vice president; Lee Adler, past president; and Reid Williamson, director. This program, accompanied by slides at the opening session, assured an outstanding experience for everyone who attended.

The 1968 National Trust meeting in Savannah had its headquarters in the auditorium that predated Savannah's Civic Center, spanning the western trust lots on Orleans Square. The delegates assembled there for major programs. Savannah's Junior League hosted a beautiful luncheon around the fountain in Forsyth Park; the Trustees Garden Club, affiliated with the Garden Club of America, sponsored a riverside luncheon below Emmett Park, an outstanding area on East Bay Street, which it had saved from the fate of a parking lot. The new DeSoto Hilton Hotel was the site of a dinner, and the annual banquet, at which Thomas Hoving, director of the Metropolitan Museum of Art, was the featured speaker, was held at the Savannah Inn and Country Club on Wilmington Island. During the banquet, James Biddle, president of the board of trustees of the National Trust, presented that organization's most prestigious award, the Crowninshield, to St. Clair Wright of Annapolis, Maryland. The Savannah meeting included a dramatic evening reception at the National Park Service's magnificent Fort Pulaski on the Savannah River near Tybee Island, where a bugler played taps as the American flag was lowered at sunset.

Those attending toured some of Savannah's outstanding houses: the Davenport House; the Owens-Thomas House and Telfair Academy of Arts and Sciences, both designed by the English architect William Jay; the Juliette Gordon Low Birthplace, National Program Center of the Girl Scouts of America; the Green-Meldrim House; and the Andrew Low House, state headquarters of the Colonial Dames. There were walking tours along Bull Street, along the riverfront, to the Trustees' Garden and St. Julian Street areas, and in the Pulaski Square/West Jones Street area redevelopment project. The Trust's 1968 annual meeting in Savannah, the largest to that date with its attendance of nine hundred, was a watershed that established a format for annual meetings continued by the Trust beyond the next decade.

Lee served as trustee of the National Trust, 1971–80, and has continued his interest as trustee emeritus to the present. Each year he is a panelist in the session "Real Estate is the Name of the Game" at the annual conference. During his affiliation with the trust since 1961, he has known and worked with executive directors and presidents Robert D. Garvey Jr., James Biddle, Michael Ainsley, Jackson Walter and Richard Moe, and with chairs David E. Finley, Gordon Gray, Carlisle Humelsine, Alan Boyd, Robert Bass, Henry Jordan and Nancy Campbell.

For his service, Lee received the National Trust's Crowninshield Award in 1982, and in 1989, President George H. W. Bush awarded him the National Medal of Arts for outstanding contribution to the nation in the field of historic preservation. President Bush presented twelve medals on Friday, November 17, 1989, at the White House. This was the fifth annual ceremony "to honor those who have encouraged the arts in this country and offered inspiration to others either through distinguished achievement, support or patronage," according to an article in the *New York Times* that day.

Lee's citation, bestowed along with an elaborate medal, recognized him for "civic leadership in preserving for all time the beauty of Savannah, Georgia, and for making that city a model of the art of historic preservation." In remarks prepared for the ceremony, Lee said: "Historic Preservation has been recognized by the President of the United States. It means that this country, a world leader in technological advancement, now considers its architectural heritage an essential element in our civilization."

The Isaiah Davenport House, 324 East State Street, dates from 1820. The house was saved by Historic Savannah Foundation as its first major project in 1955.

The William Scarbrough House, designed by William Jay in 1819, was saved by Historic Savannah Foundation in 1966. Restoration of the mansion became a major project of the Foundation from 1972 to 1976. The house was restored again in the 1990s by Mills B. Lane IV and functions today as the Ships of the Sea Museum.

(Top left) The exterior of Marshall Row (1854) at 230-244 East Oglethorpe Avenue, after it had been sold to a wrecker. Individual members of Historic Savannah Foundation purchased the land from the owner and the bricks from the wrecker in order to prevent demolition.

(Top right) Marshall Row, restored.

(Bottom left) This view from the hall of one of the deteriorated Marshall Row houses looks across Oglethorpe Avenue into the Colonial Cemetery.

Two of Historic Savannah Foundation's most dedicated Board members: Seated: Robertine (Robbie) McLendon, Executive Director of the Juliette Gordon Low Birthplace; Standing: Ethelyn Nightingale McKinnon, Curator of the Davenport House.

Here are two erstwhile Armstrong College properties: 1 West Bull Street on Monterey Square (left) and a fine house on West Gaston at Whitaker Street (right), saved from demolition by Historic Savannah Foundation.

Gordon Row houses on Gordon Street between Whitaker and Barnard Streets were threatened with demolition during Armstrong College's expansion program. The houses were spared by the College's relocation to Savannah's south side.

An article in the Savannah Evening Press, November 10, 1965, describes the Pulaski Square project as "the largest redevelopment undertaking by Historic Savannah Foundation since its founding in 1954." The inventory showed more than 100 buildings in the area, which included two blocks on West Jones Street from Whitaker to Tattnall and the entire Pulaski Ward. Here are before and after pictures of 106-108 West Harris Street.

This view across Troup Square shows the Troup trust buildings and McDonough Row in derelict condition in the early 1960s. Under Historic Savannah Foundation's leadership, the Savannah Housing Authority worked with the U.S. Department of the Interior to create one of the earliest plans to use an urban renewal conservation program.

This view shows Troup Square with a conservation sign and the Troup trust buildings before restoration.

The Oliver Sturgess House, built in 1815 on Reynolds Square, is the remaining half of a double house that was demolished in the 1930s. This exceptional house was purchased by Historic Savannah Foundation and sold to Charles H. Morris, who restored it for offices.

McDonough Row, 410-424 East Charlton Street, built in 1881 for John McDonough, was also restored. These houses are three stories of Savannah grey brick overlaid with stucco.

The Savannah delegation to the National Trust for Historic Preservation's annual conference in Philadelphia in 1966. Back row, from left: Wayne Cunningham, Robert D. Gunn, Kitty Williamson, J. Reid Williamson, Executive Director, Historic Savannah Foundation, and Lee Adler, Foundation president. Seated, from left: Peggy K. Gunn, Robertine McLendon, Director, Juliette Gordon Low Birthplace, and Emma Adler.

Elizabeth (Beth) Lattimore Reiter, staff assistant, and J. Reid Williamson, Executive Director of Historic Savannah Foundation, with Jimmy Biddle, President of the National Trust for Historic Preservation, at the National Trust's annual conference in Denver, Colorado, October 1969.

Winners of the National Medal of Arts are shown in the East Room of the White House, November 17, 1989. Lee Adler is standing between President George Bush and First Lady Barbara Bush.

SAVE THE BAY:
THE STORY OF THE HYATT HOTEL

The long process of creating Savannah's Riverfront Plaza, which was dedicated on June 3, 1977, began in the early 1960s. Many challenges existed. On the west side of City Hall, a few buildings still stood on the old wharf area along the river. One of these was a four-story building joined by a covered ramp to a building built along the bluff. A row of Victorian warehouses was connected to a building across River Street at the bend of the Savannah River. Railroad tracks along River Street linked the industries located on the west and east ends of this old part of the city. In order to take down the four-story building still standing between the railroad tracks and the Savannah River, the city considered demolishing the buildings it connected on the Bay Street level. This threat drew the attention of Historic Savannah Foundation.

The buildings the city wanted demolished were listed in Historic Savannah Foundation's published inventory. One of the owners formed a partnership with a local developer to create a hotel on the site. The mayor's River Street Committee, organized to accomplish the urban-renewal plaza plan, recommended the proposed hotel. Representatives of Historic Savannah Foundation met with the prospective developers, and in due course the Foundation's board approved plans for new construction. They accepted a design submitted by Helfrich and Grantham Architects for a hotel compatible in scale, constructed of Savannah grey brick with Belgian block quoins. Historic Savannah Foundation believed that a new building compatible with its neighbors would add to the revitalization of the area. The new hotel would replace the Victorian warehouse directly adjacent to City Hall on the west side, leaving City Hall, with its beautiful copper dome, as a perfect centerpiece for the ranges of buildings which stretched along the river to the east and west. The proposed hotel would extend along an unused street into an adjacent vacant lot. Historic Savannah Foundation made its decision to comply with the city's request for demolition because of the quality of the proposed design and the Foundation's goal to increase the vitality and economic health of downtown Savannah.

A few years later, after demolition had been completed, a new hotel plan consisting of an out-of-scale hotel and a fifteen-story tower was presented to Historic Savannah Foundation. By this time, an additional developer had joined the hotel project. Walter Hartridge, a young lawyer and cousin of the historian Walter Charlton Hartridge, was president of Historic Savannah Foundation at that time. In 1968, Lee had given up the presidency, which had become a coveted post in civic leadership. After serving four years as vice president and five years as president, he turned the office over to Robert D. Gunn, who was succeeded by Walter Hartridge. Now a building completely foreign to the proportions of those along the river, one which would tower over City Hall, was on the table. This proposal split the board and the membership of Historic Savannah Foundation.

Meetings with the developers made no progress, and in spite of the difference between previously approved plans and new ones, there was no way that this new project could be stopped. Historic Savannah Foundation's new leadership seemed to have little conscience with regard to the goals of the Foundation, and the city had no historic zoning laws. Officers and directors of the Foundation who were related by family or business interests to the developers made no effort to see that the Foundation remained true to its purpose.

As members of Historic Savannah Foundation's executive committee, we were frustrated because the organization would take no position against the proposed development. After many meetings, however, we persuaded the leadership of the Foundation to allow an expert to be brought in to give advice. Lee, who in addition to serving on Historic Savannah's executive committee was also a trustee for the National Trust for Historic Preservation, asked the National Trust to suggest someone. The trust selected John Fisher-Smith, affiliated with the nationally prominent firm Skidmore, Owings and Merrill and chair of the American Institute of Architects' design committee, to visit Savannah and make recommendations regarding the proposed hotel. Mr. Fisher-Smith recommended that no high-rise buildings be built along the riverfront or in the historic district, but rather be placed east or west of the historic district, looking into it in the way that New York's tall buildings look into Central Park.

In his report to Historic Savannah Foundation submitted after his August 1969 visit, John Fisher-Smith wrote: "It is a matter of national concern that the old Savannah Riverfront be protected so that it may be restored and developed for effective commercial use while preserving its unique historic character. To do this it will be necessary to place a 40-foot height limit along the waterfront from West Broad to East Broad Street....It is equally important that new structures along the Riverfront area be built so as to enhance and to maintain the quality of the scale and design prevalent....The choice of materials and the design and massing must be carefully handled." With regard to the proposed tower structure which has not been built at this writing, but for which an out-of-scale plan still exists, Mr. Fisher-Smith said, "The tower structure would be completely out-of-scale with the old historic structures, and if permitted, would lead to further towers along the waterfront creating a wall between the city and the river." In spite of Mr. Fisher-Smith's visit and his report, which was favorably received by the board of Historic Savannah Foundation, the Foundation, by secret vote of its executive committee, continued to support the high-rise development.

By this time, Lee was so frustrated that he became a leader in forming a new nonprofit entity called Save the Bay. He persuaded J. Frederick Waring, a prominent native Savannahian who had recently retired and returned to the city, to serve as chair. Soon they learned that Annapolis, Maryland, had a similar problem on its bay front, and they held meetings with Mrs. J. M. P. Wright, president of Historic Annapolis Foundation. After discussion with Annapolis, the decision was made to sue the developers and related parties. At this time, Save the Bay heard of an organization in San Francisco that was working to prevent high-rise buildings in inappropriate locations. From the San Francisco group, Save the Bay learned about running newspaper advertisements to show the visual effect of the objectionable project and to explain how it would hurt the city architecturally and economically by degrading the historic atmosphere along Savannah's riverfront.

The Save the Bay effort caused much ill feeling. The lawsuit was fought on the grounds that the demolished building on Bay Street had encroached on Factors' Walk, which Walter Hartridge discovered was in the public domain. After attorney Aaron Buchsbaum fought a long and successful legal battle, Save the Bay won the suit. By this time, the River Street Plaza was under construction, and a meeting took place to compromise the design of the high-rise hotel. Historic Savannah Foundation, the city administration and the developers agreed to bring in Edmund Bacon, the noted city planner from Philadelphia, for consultation. Mr. Bacon suggested a plan to lower the proposed building to nine stories so that it would not be higher than the dome of City Hall. But this plan, which was adopted, allowed the hotel to extend across River Street. This was a blow to the members of the Save the Bay committee, but there was nothing more to be done. As the building was being erected, there was much enthusiasm in City Hall and the Chamber of Commerce. But when the skin of the new hotel began to be visible, many were aghast at the inappropriate scale and materials. By then, it was too late, and the out-of-scale, out-of-place structure was completed.

Looking back on this unfortunate conflict, it is easy to see that Historic Savannah Foundation should have opposed and fought the inappropriate development. The Foundation should have purchased the site and secured a sensitive developer to design and build a suitable hotel. As it is, the present building is typical of early Hyatt hotels, a formula with an atrium which prevents many rooms' taking advantage of the site by offering views of the river. Today, although the Hyatt is a successful and popular hotel, many acknowledge its inappropriate design. In recent years, Historic Savannah Foundation has opposed high-rise plans for the still-vacant lot west of the Hyatt.

THE SCARBROUGH HOUSE RESTORATION

When the Hyatt Hotel crisis subsided, Historic Savannah Foundation faced a new challenge in 1972. The William Scarbrough House (1818) on West Broad Street is one of the outstanding American mansions of its time. Its architect, William Jay, also designed the Owens-Thomas House, Savannah's distinctive house museum of the English Regency period, and the Telfair Academy of Arts and Sciences, Savannah's fine arts museum. The Scarbrough House, which had been the setting for an elegant ball in 1819 when President James Monroe visited Savannah to assist in the ceremonies pertaining to the launching of the SS *Savannah*, had experienced a different history from that of the other two Jay houses.

Ownership passed from the Scarbroughs eventually to the Jones-DeRenne-Barrow family, which has owned Wormsloe Plantation since colonial days. In 1876, Wymberley Jones bequeathed the Scarbrough House to the public school system "to be used as a school for children of African descent." Thus, the house functioned as the West Broad Street School from 1876 until school integration in 1966. The deed then reverted to the Barrow family. Mrs. Craig Barrow gave her share to Historic Savannah Foundation, and the Foundation purchased the remaining shares from members of the family. After the Scarbrough Foundation was formed to raise money to restore the house, Historic Savannah Foundation turned the deed over to this ambitious new foundation. Through the generosity of Mrs. A. Ware Bosworth and Gertrude W. Hollowbush, the Scarbrough Foundation succeeded in raising enough money for a new roof, but by 1972, this entity admitted defeat and gave the deed back to Historic Savannah Foundation. The controversy within Historic Savannah Foundation over the construction of the Hyatt Hotel had dealt an almost lethal blow, but the Scarbrough House provided the challenge that would heal some of the wounds.

At this time, Mrs. Elliot Cobb was president of Historic Savannah Foundation, which after eighteen years had succeeded in stabilizing the historic fabric within the National Historic District without putting significant funds into the restoration of individual buildings. By 1972, over eight hundred buildings had been restored, and historic preservation was in the mainstream. Historic zoning legislation, for which enabling legislation had been successfully obtained at the state level in the 1960s, was passed that year in local referendum with a three-to-one majority voting for it. A sad footnote is that the vote came just too late to save the superb Odd Fellows Hall, with its elaborate terra cotta decoration, on Telfair Square at the northwest corner of State and Barnard Streets; two fine little mid-nineteenth-century buildings on Johnson Square which were demolished by the expansion of Savannah Bank (now the National Bank of Commerce); and a free-standing Italianate residence on the southwest corner of Hall and Abercorn, which gave way to an optical shop at the back of the lot with an unsightly parking lot on Hall Street. By then, Savannah was reaping the benefits of a booming tourist industry.

Under Kay Cobb's leadership, Historic Savannah Foundation took on the task of restoring the Scarbrough House. Kay asked Emma to come on the board after the Hyatt Hotel crisis to serve as chair of the Scarbrough House restoration project. Her respect for Kay Cobb allowed Emma to return to Historic Savannah's board. The Scarbrough House restoration committee hired John Milner, restoration architect, of Chadds Ford, Pennsylvania, to direct the restoration efforts. Tony Adams became the general contractor.

Reid Williamson left Savannah, after seven years of outstanding leadership as Historic Savannah Foundation's executive director, to take a statewide job in historic preservation in Indianapolis, Indiana. Reid, who has headed the Historic Landmarks Foundation of Indiana since the mid-1970s, says he just created little "Historic Savannahs" throughout the state of Indiana. Today, Reid Williamson is one of the most respected historic preservationists in the United States.

Decoursey McIntosh, of Pittsburgh, Pennsylvania, became the new director of the Foundation in 1973. Mrs. Lawrence Lee succeeded Kay Cobb as president. Under Betty Lee's leadership, the Foundation raised the necessary funds—more than a million dollars—to restore the Scarbrough House. Mills B. Lane made a significant contribution with the proviso (which the Foundation accepted) that the third floor, added in 1843 by Godfrey Barnsley, son-in-law of William Scarbrough, be removed. The J. Bulow Campbell Foundation in Atlanta matched Lane's contribution.

When the Scarbrough House opened in 1976, the front rooms with curved ends flanking the newly marbleized atrium contained decorative arts exhibitions of the period of the house, installed for the Foundation by Page Talbot of Philadelphia. Panels in the halls outlined the house's history, including its years as a public school.

Historic Savannah Foundation's plans did not include period furnishings to make the building into another house museum. It would be used instead to illuminate the genius of William Jay and to point out architectural similarities and differences in the design of Savannah's three existing William Jay houses open to the public. It was the hope of the Foundation's leadership that administration of the Scarbrough House could be turned over to the trustees of the Telfair Academy, who also served as administrators for the Owens-Thomas House.

Historic Savannah Foundation moved its offices from the Davenport House to the Scarbrough House in 1976, and the Junior League of Savannah also leased office space on the ground floor. The parlor floor was open to the public and available for receptions and meetings.

In the early 1990s, Mills B. Lane IV provided funding to allow the Telfair Academy to purchase the Scarbrough House and to permit Historic Savannah Foundation to move its offices to Broughton Street, Savannah's main commercial street, which was in dire need of revitalization. At that time, the Junior League relocated its offices to the carriage houses behind the Andrew Low House. Prior to Mills Lane's gift, the Telfair Academy had purchased property on Telfair Square for a new facility for exhibitions, educational programs, and storage. Although the Telfair trustees accepted Lane's gift in February 1991, years passed and the Telfair was unable to create a viable use for the house in its management plans. In 1994, Mills Lane IV gained possession of the Scarbrough House, and it reopened in 1997, superbly restored as the Ships of the Sea Museum, a new and expertly organized home for his late father's model ship collection.

THE MASSIE HERITAGE INTERPRETATION CENTER
AS TOLD BY EMMA ADLER

I decided to run for election to the Savannah– Chatham County Board of Public Education in 1974. Elected to represent District I in 1975, I served a four-year term which ended in 1979.

The Massie School, Savannah's oldest public school, which opened in 1856, had closed as an elementary school at the end of the 1974 school year. The school administration considered its pupil population too small to be cost- effective. Marilyn Franklin had been the last principal of the integrated student body. In 1975, Saxon Bargeron, one of Savannah's outstanding educators, a veteran teacher in both public and private schools who had served also as superintendent of the public school system, was assigned to Massie to conduct research on the school's history. Her office was in the school's western wing on the ground floor.

Since the Massie School was in my district, the board of education appointed me to head a committee to develop long-range plans for the old school. This became the Friends of Massie committee, on which I still serve. I was particularly happy to chair this committee because my father and Lee's father had attended Massie School as young boys. Saxon Bargeron became a strong member of the Friends of Massie committee, which included representation from the board of education, the school administration and the general public. We met once a month during the school year and called meetings as necessary. We developed a long-range plan with restoration of the building as a top priority. The board of education set aside $5,000 for the consulting services of an architect and chose Robert D. Gunn, a past president of Historic Savannah Foundation, from ten applicants. The Friends of Massie committee envisioned a meaningful program of instruction: a heritage education program staffed with a lead teacher who could work with classroom teachers and students K–12 from public and private schools. The Friends of Massie committee also recognized the importance of persuading the school administration to put the building back on scheduled maintenance at the level provided to all schools. Restoration costs above and beyond regular maintenance would be borne by the Friends of Massie committee.

Through Mrs. Bargeron's efforts, the school, designed by John Norris, whose work in Savannah includes the Green-Meldrim House, the Custom House, the Andrew Low House and more, was listed on the National Register of Historic Places. Mrs. Bargeron also secured a grant from Georgia's State

Historic Preservation Office to reproduce the school's original front doors, for which adequate photographic and design information was available. The committee raised and the State Historic Preservation Office matched funds to re-stucco the building. The school system funded and installed a new roof after the committee succeeded in its effort to get the building back on the maintenance schedule.

The school administration assigned a teacher in 1977 to inaugurate the heritage education program envisioned by the Friends of Massie committee. This was Sarah Parsons, an outstanding elementary school teacher. Mrs. Parsons, a natural for the job, had been taking her students on field trips all around Savannah's historic district to explain the city's unique and special character. "Visual literacy" became a goal, and, as a result, a built-in constituency of historic preservationists was created.

The Friends of Massie committee, securing grants from the National Endowment for the Arts, the Hodge Foundation, the Women of Christ Church, the Lane Foundation and the Georgia Endowment for the Humanities, continued to pursue its goals to put permanent teaching installations into the building. These exhibitions would be the textbooks of the heritage education program, providing important information on Savannah's city plan, her heritage of eighteenth- and nineteenth-century architecture, and her socioeconomic history. James W. (Jim) Morton III was the superb designer of Massie's exhibitions, and I worked at his side creating their formats.

The architecture installation funded by the National Endowment for the Arts illustrates the Egyptian, Greek, Roman, Gothic and International styles outstanding in the history of Western civilization. The elements of these styles are related to important examples of each style found in Savannah.

The Victorian installation, funded by the Hodge Foundation and the Women of Christ Church, contains artifacts from such tragic losses as the City Market, the DeSoto Hotel, Odd Fellows Hall and the Union Station. It shows pictures of the destroyed buildings as well as of the buildings that replaced them. The city plan installation, funded by the Georgia Endowment for the Humanities, has as its centerpiece a three-dimensional model of Savannah's National Historic District, crafted by Jim Morton. On the walls in logical progression are illustrations, maps and drawings depicting the development of the ancient gridiron plan from Greece to Rome to the British Isles to this country. The growth of the city of Savannah from its founding in 1733 until 1856, when land owned by the city was fully developed, is also displayed. This installation, which features the research of Professor John Reps of Cornell University, provides an excellent orientation to Savannah's National Historic District.

Massie's Heritage Education Program coordinated student participation in Historic Savannah Foundation's annual Georgia Day celebration from 1978 until 1997, when the Georgia Historical Society replaced Historic Savannah Foundation as the sponsoring organization. The school system's role in this celebration had been raised to the level of co-sponsorship with Historic Savannah Foundation in 1982, and the name was changed to the Georgia Heritage Celebration. During my term on the board of education, 1975–79, I encouraged greater school participation in what by that time had become Georgia Week. A program for students from the public and private schools in Savannah and Chatham County was coordinated at all grade levels through the heritage education program at the Massie Heritage Interpretation Center. At the elementary schools, art teachers encouraged drawings of the colonial period featuring General Oglethorpe; his ship, the *Anne*, which brought the colonists to Savannah; Chief Tomochichi, a good friend of the colonists; Mary Musgrove, his interpreter; and other subjects.

As a board of education member, I had attended a program at Wilder Middle School, sponsored by the social studies department, which featured during an assembly an expert impersonator of Teddy Roosevelt describing to the student body his achievements as president of the United States. This activity gave me an idea for a middle school program during Georgia Week.

At the middle school level, town meeting assemblies featuring a prominent person in Georgia's history were inaugurated and offered as a lively approach to instruction. The volunteers who visited the schools in costume had studied the lives of the featured luminary, and teachers assured that students were well versed in the accomplishments of this important person. The character of the year, who has represented many ethnic groups, was given widespread visibility and was known throughout the community because of newspaper and television coverage. There was also publicity about the volunteers who gave their time to portray the characters. On February 12, the honored character for the year would march with General Oglethorpe, Chief Tomochichi, and Mary Musgrove in the elementary schools' procession of over four thousand students down Bull Street from Forsyth Park to City Hall. At the high school level, selected SEARCH (gifted) students were taken on special tours of the downtown area conducted by volunteers from the Friends of Massie committee. The costumed characters were also featured at the Georgia Day luncheon, which from 1982 to 1997 was co-sponsored by Historic Savannah Foundation and the Chatham–Savannah Public Schools. A constituency of young people who care about their city's history was renewed each year during this annual celebration.

The annual May Day Celebration, which had originated in Calhoun

Square in front of the school in the 1850s and continued for about a hundred years, was revived and coordinated through Massie's heritage education program to bring a colorful student festival back to the square each year at the beginning of May. The heritage education program also conducts staff development workshops to instruct teachers in Savannah's economic, social and architectural history.

The Friends of Massie committee added a representative from Savannah Country Day School and sought advice, when necessary, from the history department at Armstrong State College and the National Trust for Historic Preservation. Dr. Antoinette Lee, the Trust's education consultant and an advisor to the committee, is credited with the name Massie Heritage Interpretation Center. Since the transfer of Sarah Parsons to Gadsden Elementary School in 1987, the following teachers have served capably at Massie: Frances Smith,Marva Harris, Lyn McDonald, Roger Smith, Neely Saturday and Leah McGriff. Larry Smith is the Heritage Education Teacher at this printing.

The public school administration's chain of command for Massie has always come through social studies. Candy Lowe, the current administrator, is dedicated to the importance of Massie's programs and has enhanced the center's standing with the board of education and the superintendent's administrative team. Recently the board has initiated the process with the U.S. Department of the Interior to seek landmark status for Massie.

The Massie Center has received awards from the National Association of State and Local History and the American Institute of Architects, and, in 1987, received a Governor's Award in the Humanities. Massie's most recent teaching installation, "The Debatable Lands: Native Americans in Coastal Georgia," opened in January 2003. This installation, co-sponsored with the board of the Savannah Science Museum and the Coastal Heritage Society, tells the story of the indigenous population that greeted James E. Oglethorpe in 1733. It includes artifacts from archaeological digs conducted in Savannah during the 1930s, and is an important part of instruction at the eighth-grade level.

SAVANNAH LANDMARK REHABILITATION PROJECT
AS TOLD BY LEE ADLER

The push to restore the neglected and often abandoned buildings in the old part of Savannah took twenty years (1955–75). During this period, over eight hundred buildings were rescued from demolition. As the tourist business grew dramatically, Savannah's central core became a recognized asset.

Prices had begun to rise, and prospective owners were looking for more reasonably priced historic properties. Access to downtown, with its vital business district, was quick and easy from Ardsley Park, a suburb built after World War I, and also from several additional communities built after World War II when many people fled downtown to live in the suburbs. As people went downtown to work or shop (the main commercial street, Broughton Street, was still alive although declining), they drove through an area called the Victorian District without looking to the left or right at its handsome, though dilapidated, wooden structures. The Victorian District was Savannah's first streetcar suburb, started in the 1870s after development of the public land (which today forms the older National Historic Landmark District) had been completed. Most of the buildings in the older district were built of brick after two severe fires destroyed many early wooden buildings.

During the 1870s and 1880s, Savannah's first suburb was coming to life. Unlike the historic district, it had no squares because of the unwillingness of the city fathers to forego tax revenues by creating public land for parks or squares. So the Victorian District was laid out in a simple grid pattern with rather large, deep lots and lanes between the blocks. The new area contained many carpenter-built houses of wood because paved streets and public transportation had reduced the fire hazard. Wooden construction was cheaper than brick construction. This first suburb was occupied mostly by middle-income working people.

In the 1950s and 1960s, the Department of Housing and Urban Development concentrated on a nationwide slum clearance program called urban renewal. It was thought that new government-assisted housing developments would revitalize cities and provide better housing There was also a push to create new commercial areas where deteriorated housing had existed before slum clearance. In Savannah, on the west side, where decrepit shacks had existed to house a low-income African American population, a commercial urban renewal project took place. This removed a substantial number of black families from their homes just as whites, lured by the considerable incentive of FHA loans, were moving away from the Victorian District to the suburbs. The Victorian District then filled with low-income renters from West Broad Street's Yamacraw area. Slum landlords sometimes owned as many as four hundred apartment units in properties ranging from one hundred to two hundred buildings. Concern about the area developed among the experienced preservationists who had dealt earlier with reclaiming the National Historic District. This time the problem had an added dimension—people.

The preservation movement launched by Historic Savannah Foundation in 1955 was concerned with the saving of important vacant buildings slated for demolition. The Victorian District, however, presented a vastly different problem, because a large population, neglected by the city and the housing authority, was living there in substandard conditions. The only interest of slumlords or absentee landlords was the income from the rental properties. Slumlords would abandon buildings rather than make repairs and/or pay taxes if the cost was too great to put the building in sound condition. Since there were no organized tenant associations, inhabitants of the Victorian District were at the mercy of the slumlords, whose purpose was to turn a profit. If adequate city ordinances existed, they were not enforced. However, many abandoned buildings were destroyed.

Since I had intimate knowledge of Arthur Ziegler's work in Pittsburgh revitalizing the historic Manchester neighborhood, I tried to interest Historic Savannah Foundation in using his techniques to bring back Savannah's Victorian District. Buildings currently occupied by low-income renters would be improved for them, and the restoration of available, freestanding Victorian houses by prospective individual homeowners would be promoted. This effort met with no success.

Following my failure to interest Historic Savannah Foundation in this new dimension of work in the Victorian District, I encouraged a local investment banking firm to work with a real estate development company in Boston to improve low-income housing in the Victorian District. This effort was stalled by the demise of the federal government's Model Cities Program in 1972. However, during this effort, Savannah Landmark had taken options with renewable clauses on a handsome row of Victorian houses.

I formed the Savannah Landmark Rehabilitation Project with a group of interested Savannahians in order to come to grips with the problem in the Victorian District. Before the organization was incorporated, investigation in the area indicated that most units were rented by responsible people who were good housekeepers unable to afford home ownership. Many of them had been there for ten to fifteen years, and some had lived there even longer.

Deterioration in the Victorian District was steady. But the area was blessed with good shade trees; the streets were paved; and the Victorian houses were wonderful. Proximity to downtown and to Forsyth Park was an added attraction.

The Savannah Landmark Rehabilitation Project was incorporated in July 1974, and the options that had been taken out earlier were given to this new nonprofit organization. This was not a membership organization. Instead it consisted of a diverse group whose interest was to deal with the problems of the inhabitants and the deteriorating buildings in the Victorian District. Beth Lattimore Reiter, a former staff member of Historic Savannah Foundation who had conducted an inventory of the Victorian housing stock in the eight-hundred-acre area, became the first director of the Savannah Landmark Rehabilitation Project in 1977. This area of twelve hundred housing units was listed on the National Register of Historic Places in 1974 with east-west boundaries at Price and Montgomery Streets. In 1984, the east-west boundaries were extended to East Broad and Martin Luther King, Jr. Boulevard.

Savannah Landmark began with a board of eighteen. Soon the number increased to twenty-five members representing a cross-section of Savannah's citizens, all of whom had the primary interest of finding a way to accomplish decent, safe, sanitary housing for the "responsible poor" in the beautiful Victorian District. The board debated about directing its focus on home ownership or on rental housing. Both ideas were thoroughly explored during consultations with residents of the area. The decision was made to concentrate on rental housing, since under home ownership, as conditions improved and prices of property increased, inhabitants might sell their units. Under the rental plan, Savannah Landmark would control the property, take the risks involved, and respond to maintenance problems which had been ignored by the slum landlords. Savannah Landmark proposed to provide decent housing for people who needed it.

Savannah Landmark first approached the National Endowment for the Arts, Architecture Section. Robert McNulty, its energetic director, came to Savannah to assess the projected program of Savannah Landmark. Having decided that the vision of the organization could provide a national model for low-income housing in historic districts, the endowment provided an initial $17,000 matching grant for staff and an operating budget.

A pilot project was selected: three houses on Price Street near the Victorian District, which qualified for urban renewal funds, were purchased. Working with the Housing Authority of Savannah, through which federal funds could pass, Savannah Landmark applied successfully through the city for a $100,000 Comprehensive Employment Training Act (CETA) grant. William Mobley, an experienced general contractor, was then hired as project supervisor. He employed fourteen young people, many from the neighborhood, and trained them in carpentry, sheet rock installation, internal demolition and more. The mechanical elements were subcontracted to experienced firms. Mr. Mobley was a gifted and serious person who was anxious to train young blacks in sustaining job skills. He instructed them twice a week, at night, at a school established by minority contractors. Under its Economic Opportunity Authority, the city had a program called "Operation Diploma," which trained young people in housing maintenance skills while they completed the requirements for a high school diploma. Ronald Roberts, who availed himself of this opportunity, became Savannah Landmark's maintenance supervisor.

Savannah Landmark obtained additional options in the Victorian District so that when the program began to expand and prices escalated, it would be able to purchase buildings at reasonable prices. Bob McNulty introduced Savannah Landmark to the Urban Reinvestment Task Force, which referred it to the Ford Foundation, for which low-income housing was a high priority. Savannah Landmark also presented its ideas and goals to various sections of the federal government's Housing and Urban Development Department.

As work on the three Price Street houses progressed, Savannah Landmark had something to show, and the partnerships that it was developing were beginning to be impressive. Mr. Mobley and his crew were hard at work transforming three semi-detached units—a splendid architectural row. Donald Naismith, director of Savannah's Housing Authority, became a vital part of the program by smoothing and lessening bureaucratic paperwork at all levels.

Savannah Landmark approached the Carver State Bank, Savannah's premier minority bank. With notes cosigned by a few Savannah Landmark board members, $180,000 was secured to buy options, produce sales contracts, and renovate buildings. As a principal officer of this bank, Joseph N. Bell came on the board, as did Judge Eugene Gadsden, who was a bank director. This bank's help, which was obtained because Savannah Landmark was working to uplift its constituency, enabled the board to approach other major banks as additional banking dollars were needed.

Savannah Landmark hosted a national conference in Savannah in December 1977 to address the problems of deterioration and displacement which were occurring in architecturally stable inner-city neighborhoods across the United States. Leaders of two other innovative projects in Pittsburgh, Pennsylvania, and Cincinnati, Ohio, joined to co-sponsor the conference. Grants for the conference were made by the National Endowment for the Arts, the National Trust for Historic Preservation, and Partners for Livable Places (a coalition of organizations to improve the built environment, now headed by Bob McNulty). The planning committee invited preservationists and federal, regional and local governments throughout the country to address the specific issues of funding, management, design, and low-income housing rehabilitation.

Four hundred participants from thirty-eight states attended the conference. Its work sessions were held in and around the Victorian District in schools, churches, and neighborhood public places. Tours illustrated the problems in Savannah and highlighted Savannah Landmark's effort to address them. Speakers discussed the latest and most successful approaches to solving low-income housing problems. A tremendous amount of enthusiasm was generated. As a result, HUD, the Ford Foundation, and the National Trust for Historic Preservation gave help to continue Savannah Landmark's mission, and sixty-four units of Section 8 Substantial Rehabilitation Rent Subsidies Set Aside were made to Savannah Landmark from HUD. The rental subsidy was the key element to help low-income renters secure rehabilitated housing. The Section 8 federal subsidy, when added to the rent paid by the tenant, produced a fair rental fee to the project owner, in this case the Savannah Landmark Rehabilitation Project Inc.

The 1977 Landmark Conference was noted for the participation of nationally prominent figures who were leading the effort to improve low-income housing and to assist low-income residents by preventing their displacement from their neighborhoods. Attending the conference, in addition to Robert McNulty, who helped with its planning and promotion, were Nancy Hanks, chair of the National Endowment for the Arts; James Biddle, president of the National Trust for Historic Preservation; Carl Westmoreland, director of the Mt. Auburn Good Housing Corporation Cincinnati; Arthur Ziegler, president of the Pittsburgh History and Landmarks Foundation; Richard Fleming, an assistant secretary of HUD; and many HUD officials, both from Washington and from HUD regional headquarters in Atlanta. Mayor John Rousakis of Savannah and many from his city administration and the housing authority also participated. The Ford Foundation was present and extended its interest with additional grants. Edmund Bacon, noted urban planner of Philadelphia, spoke eloquently on the wrong-headed vision of the urban renewal program, so popular in the 1960s, and proclaimed this conference to be the finest he had ever attended.

The HUD rent subsidies allowed Savannah Landmark to expand its activities considerably, and all of Savannah's banks helped finance the purchase of optioned properties. Mr. Mobley enlarged his operations, and Loy Veal, who had managed a housing project in Savannah, became the new director of Landmark. The decision was made to have Savannah Landmark become a nonprofit housing developer.

The news media became interested in Savannah Landmark's programs, and many newspaper articles and television programs provided excellent publicity. All of this was helpful in securing funding.

On August 1, 1978, Savannah Landmark entered into a so-called "Innovative Project": the completion in eighteen months of sixty-four units obtained from HUD. At the end of the year, the Urban Reinvestment Task Force provided an administrative grant with valuable technical assistance in producing work programs and management plans to assist this project.

The Innovative Project began with the rehabilitation of units on Bolton Street. The Georgia Department of Natural Resources Historic Preservation Division and the U.S. Department of the Interior jointly provided the salary of Eric DeLony, architect with the Historic American Engineering Record, National Park Service, who with his family moved to Savannah to design the project working with the local architectural firm Lominak, Jewett and Spenser. During his tenure, the Historic American Buildings Survey (HABS) continued the work started in the 1930s by documenting a selection of the houses in the Victorian District and preparing a comprehensive history of the neighborhood.

The Ford Foundation's interest continued with the provision of grant monies for property holding and emergency maintenance of unrestored units. An extremely important Ford Foundation contribution to Savannah Landmark was a letter of intent to help finance the purchase of over 250 units for an expanded project.

It was realized that with sixty-four units underway in the Victorian District and the three units on Price Street, Savannah Landmark would have to acquire many more units to prevent the major displacement of residents in the area. Savannah Landmark also discovered an important landlord whose properties needed upgrading and would be eligible for housing subsidies. HUD suggested that Savannah Landmark apply through the city for a Neighborhood Strategy Area (NSA) for the Victorian District. This enabled HUD to award the city five hundred Section 8 substantial rehabilitation units. At first, the city wanted to use these valuable vouchers all over the city, but HUD insisted that all should be concentrated in the Victorian District to create a visible positive result. Savannah Landmark made a big mistake at this time. Wanting to be agreeable with the city and not wanting to shun the city's own housing department, Savannah Landmark asked the city for only half the awarded units, which had to be rehabilitated in six years.

The city had set up its own housing authority using approximately $4 million of Block Grant Funds. The mayor, John Rousakis, had been instrumental in securing a good amount of these funds, since he had been head of the League of Cities, quite an accomplishment for a mayor of a city of 150,000. The city manager, who really ran the city government, had set up a housing division within his purview. The city manager took 250 units, and after the required six years, when Savannah Landmark completed its 250 units and needed more, the organization found out that the city had used only 50 units and returned 200 units to HUD without informing Savannah Landmark. This was a tragedy of major proportions to Savannah Landmark and, of course, to the Victorian District and its residents.

The city manager, a conscientious person, believed all decisions should be channeled through him. As a private nonprofit entity, Savannah Landmark had worked directly with HUD through its own devices and had received about $3 million in housing grants. Now Savannah Landmark could no longer get direct help from HUD, but was required to apply through the city. It was no doubt a good thing that Savannah Landmark had been able to work with HUD, for the city at that time had paid little attention to the plight of the low-income citizens in the Victorian District.

In December 1978, as a direct result of Savannah Landmark's first successful housing conference, First Lady Rosalyn Carter visited the project. This was a great and remarkable day for Savannah Landmark, for the visit put a national spotlight on its program and emphasized citizen efforts to help solve critical housing problems. After visiting the project, Mrs. Carter participated in a panel held on a platform erected in Bolton Street in front of a row of rehabilitated houses. William Mobley, Eric DeLony and Mayor Rousakis accompanied Mrs. Carter on her visit.

Mrs. Carter talked with the CETA workers and asked them what they were doing and what the jobs meant to them. One of the workers told her he thought the project was good for the neighborhood, good for the tenants, and good for the workers. In fact, he said, he felt like a magician, and Mrs. Carter told him that the remarkable transformation from decrepit to renewed housing proved that he was, indeed, a magician. Mrs. Carter's visit was important: 250 people from Washington, Atlanta, and neighboring towns joined 250 people from Savannah to discuss Savannah Landmark's problems. It was a day to be remembered.

A side incident occurred when, a few days before her arrival, as president of Savannah Landmark, I went to see the mayor to ask him to tour the project on Bolton Street. Mayor Rousakis was going to Washington just before Mrs. Carter's visit and had been invited to return to Savannah on the First Lady's plane. Mayor Rousakis showed reluctance to visit the project, but I pointed out that it would be difficult to talk with Mrs. Carter about the project if he had not seen it.

When the mayor saw the activity in progress on Bolton Street, he became so excited that he asked Mr. Mobley to call all the workers together. He then gave an enthusiastic impromptu talk saying this was the greatest project he had ever seen. From that moment on, Savannah Landmark's projects were visited by every out-of-town official, and the mayor became an avid Landmark supporter.

There were additional property purchases in 1979 with a grant from the National Trust for Historic Preservation's Revolving Loan Fund, and negotiations were begun with the largest landlord in the district for the purchase of 261 units. Although the Innovative Project would be completed using a combination of 312 program loans and Section 8 subsidies, this financial model would not be allowed on any future projects since HUD now viewed this model as a double subsidy. In the long run, the 312 program was phased out, and thus it was evident that a new financial model would have to be developed. The Ford Foundation sent consultants to meet with Landmark, the Urban Reinvestment Task Force, and Federal National Mortgage Association (FNMA) to create a new financial model.

The fact that the Victorian District had been placed on the National Register of Historic Places enabled property owners to take advantage of the tax benefits provided by the National Historic Preservation Act of 1981. This act provided for a maximum 25 percent investment tax credit for the sensitive rehabilitation of income-producing, certified historic properties (those located within historic districts or listed on the National Register). While Savannah Landmark as a nonprofit could not directly benefit from these provisions, it could benefit from the revenues produced by a syndication model.

In February 1980, Savannah Landmark was introduced to the Cranston Companies of Ohio by the Ford Foundation consultants. Negotiations were begun on the creation of a limited partnership. Investors in the partnership would contribute capital to the venture in return for a share of the investment tax credits generated by the rehabilitation of certified historic property in the Victorian District. Landmark, the nonprofit, limited partner, would receive a share of the syndication proceeds, which would help to create an endowment for the organization to ensure its self-sufficiency. Landmark's board also realized that syndication with an experienced company would improve Landmark's ability to secure loans for the renovation of the 261 units that it was in the process of buying. After the limited partnership had been created, Savannah Landmark had the good fortune to work with Georgia's historic preservation officer, Dr. Elizabeth Lyon, who with her fine staff in Atlanta always guided us appropriately in our effort to meet state standards for rehabilitation.

The Ford Foundation provided the acquisition loan needed for the purchase of the 261 units in early 1980. However, Ford also required the City of Savannah's participation in the loan to Landmark. The city lent Savannah Landmark the entire $1.6-million-dollar purchase price from its Community Development Block Grant funds, and then Ford assumed $750,000 of the loan from the city. The purchase price of the 261-unit package, at $6,250 a unit, was an indication of the real estate market's upturn already occurring in the Victorian District as a result of Landmark's efforts.

The units were then packaged into phases. Eighty-nine original units were subdivided into a one-hundred-unit Savannah Neighborhood Action Project 1 (SNAP 1) phase. Eighty-nine units were packaged for SNAP II, and forty-four units of new construction went into SNAP III.

Then followed twenty-three months of delay. From June 1980, negotiations were carried on with HUD to receive approval for the Section 221 D-4 mortgage insurance for the projects. The problems that were ultimately solved included HUD's concern with Landmark's financial capacity and concern that a proposed local minority construction firm lacked the necessary resources to carry out all three SNAP projects.

Firm commitment by HUD followed a change in the Landmark/Cranston syndication roles. Robert C. Kanuth, the head of the Cranston Companies, agreed to be the general partner in June 1981, and the ADC Construction Company, an Atlanta-based construction firm with a track record in HUD projects, became the general contractor for all three SNAP projects. The local firm, the Polote Corporation, became the major subcontractor.

The twenty-three-month delay while these problems were being worked out caused fiscal and management problems for Landmark. Landmark and the city housing department had been required under the Uniform Relocation Act to vacate the SNAP apartments in the summer of 1980. The subsequent loss of rent and threat of vandalism and fire were of immense concern to Landmark. The Unitarian Universalist Church in Savannah supported Landmark with a grant during this holding period which enabled Landmark to hire additional maintenance personnel.

The culmination of eight years of work was finally realized on May 15, 1982, when the closing for SNAP I was held in Atlanta. A "Paint the Column" groundbreaking ceremony was held in Savannah on the 300 block of East Anderson Street, and the row of houses in this block was christened "Rousakis Row" in honor of the mayor of Savannah. Closings for SNAP II and III soon followed, bringing the total number of Landmark housing units to three hundred, or 20 percent of the housing stock in the Victorian District.

In December 1982, Savannah Landmark and the City of Savannah accepted HUD's National Recognition Award for "national excellence for partici-pation in the Victorian District Projects and for successfully using the Community Development Block Grant Programs to generate an exemplary public-private partnership in their community and serving as a worthy model for other communities." Mayor John Rousakis said, "This has been the most rewarding project in preservation in Savannah. It has assisted low income families while at the same time preserving a significant portion of Savannah's heritage. I have supported Savannah Landmark since it began. Its work has been a major thrust to improve the quality of life for our citizens. I take every mayor and city official to see this wonderful work of rehabilitation that con-cerns people."

RECENT DEVELOPMENTS AND
AN ADMONITION FOR THE FUTURE

More than two thousand people attended the National Trust for Historic Preservation's annual conference in Savannah in 1998, thirty years after the Trust's former largest annual meeting, also here, in 1968. During these thirty years, Savannah's National Historic District retained its special environment with only a few incompatible intrusions. Tourists from all over the world, now numbering about six million a year, visit the city, enjoying the squares, monuments, churches and historic buildings which are reminiscent of earlier days although they are well adapted to use by the current population.

City and county officials are aware of the impact of the preservation movement on the tourist industry and are wary of losing historic district designation because of inappropriate new construction. In 1994, the federal government proposed a monolithic annex to the courthouse which involved the destruction of two blocks of good buildings between Bull and Whitaker and Broughton and State Streets. Historic Savannah Foundation led a successful effort to locate the project in an area which would not threaten the historic fabric of the city and would insure construction in proper scale to the surrounding buildings. Guidelines for appropriate new construction within the National Historic District, commissioned by the National Trust for Historic Preservation and Historic Savannah Foundation and prepared by Christopher Chadbourne of Boston, were approved by city council in 1997 as a local ordinance. Still, public opinion is not always on the side of preservation, and the need for attention to proposed development remains constant. The fragility of Savannah's National Historic District is not universally recognized, and it is sometimes difficult, even for those who care about the city, to realize that buildings in the wrong scale and materials erode the quality of the city and will adversely affect its special atmosphere.

The project to save the important Central of Georgia Railroad Shop complex in the northwest quadrant of the old city has been ongoing since the mid-1970s. Under the direction of Eric DeLony, who now heads the National Park Service's Historic American Engineering Record, a team of young architects recorded the buildings during the summer of 1975. Beth Reiter served as architectural historian for the project, which was, at the time, threatened for its huge supply of Savannah grey bricks. The complex was eventually stabilized and was one of the first industrial properties in the South to receive National

Historic Landmark designation in 1978.

The Coastal Heritage Society has been the City of Savannah's managing entity of the Railroad Shop Complex since 1989. The Society's talented and effective director, Scott W. Smith, has been dedicated to the development of the shops. He has adaptively used the property as an industrial heritage museum and is currently engaging the community in an effort to save a significant adjoining Revolutionary War battlesite as a park to enhance the area.

By the mid-1980s, the City of Savannah recognized the need to hire a preservation officer. Beth Lattimore Reiter, who had early experience on the staff of Historic Savannah Foundation and who had served as director of the Savannah Landmark Rehabilitation project, was the city's wise choice for this position in 1986. Today, she has a staff assistant and her department is recognized as having tremendous importance, as its concerns include demolition, zoning changes, and new building within the city's historic districts.

Savannah's African American population during the first half of the twentieth century lived not only in neighborhoods on the east and west sides of Savannah but also in carriage houses and in lanes scattered throughout the old city. All of downtown Savannah could have been considered "inner city" until after World War II. By the 1990s, however, the old city looked more prosperous, although it retained its old-world charm. The squares were landscaped and well maintained by the city's Park and Tree Commission. Live oaks and magnolias still provided luxuriant shade. Fine church buildings with their traditional African American congregations endure today in downtown Savannah, and the city's diversity is recognized and appreciated.

Westley W. Law, a leading citizen and serious preservationist, was a nationally prominent member of the NAACP and leader of Savannah's civil rights movement. Mr. Law, supported by caring members of the community, spearheaded the restoration of Savannah's King-Tisdale Cottage museum, created the local Association of African American Life and History, designed its Negro Heritage Tour, and worked hard to assure the restoration of the Beach Institute Museum and to have Ulysses Davis's nationally acclaimed folk art collection housed here. With assistance from Michael Terry, who co-chaired the fund drive, Mr. Law raised $350,000 to purchase this collection. Mr. Law's most recent achievement is the creation of the Ralph Mark Gilbert Civil Rights Museum. In this fine old bank building, the story of Savannah's civil rights movement is documented in well-planned exhibits.

Broughton Street, Savannah's main commercial street, suffered serious decline from the late 1950s through the 1980s as Maas Brothers Department Store and J. C. Penney moved to shopping malls on the south side. During this period, our redevelopment effort, "Back to Broughton," proved unsuccessful.

Today, Broughton Street is undergoing significant revitalization along with Martin Luther King, Jr. Boulevard, a commercial corridor for black Savannahians during the first half of the twentieth century. These two commercial streets are evolving into areas combining commercial, cultural, and residential uses under the leadership of the Savannah Development and Renewal Authority. The completed restorations of the Lucas Theatre, built in 1921, and the Marshall House Hotel, as well as the old Kress building on Broughton Street, have changed the street. Today, Starbucks, the GAP, and Banana Republic are thriving on Broughton, along with many small businesses and restaurants.

The Lucas Theatre, an outstanding neoclassical movie palace boasting a stage that will accommodate Broadway performances, was built by Arthur Lucas in 1921 at a cost of $400,000. The theater came to Lee's attention in 1986, during our Back to Broughton project. Recognizing an irreplaceable treasure in the Lucas, Lee secured the property with an initial payment on an option to buy and called together the group which would become the Lucas Theatre for the Arts. This nonprofit entity, incorporated in 1987, undertook a multimillion-dollar project that would span a decade. Serving as presidents of the Lucas board were Emma Adler, 1986–88; Elizabeth Oxnard, 1988–92; Carolyn Stillwell, 1992–93; and Benjamin Oxnard, 1993–96. Arthur Lucas's grandson, Mills Fleming, guided the last phase of this restoration and continued as chair of the theater's board of directors until 2002. The restored Lucas is Savannah's most ambitious private restoration effort to provide cultural enrichment and entertainment.

The Savannah College of Art and Design, founded by Paula and Richard Rowan and her parents, Paul and May Poetter, has provided Savannah's outstanding source of downtown redevelopment and energy since its beginning in 1979. The College bought and restored the Guard's Armory on Bull Street at Charlton Street as well as abandoned public school buildings, an old people's home, the old county jail, warehouses, railroad and commercial buildings, an Art Deco theater and more, to make about fifty restorations within the National Historic District. The College, which had an enrollment of seventy-nine during its first year, now houses and instructs over five thousand students. Since its founding, the restoration efforts of the College, together with the economic uplift and vitality provided by the student population and administration, constitute the single most significant benefit to Savannah's National Historic District in recent years. The College put a floor under the downtown rental real estate market, and streets became safer as students populated them at all hours. In 1994, the Savannah College of Art and Design received an Honor Award from the National Trust for Historic Preservation. The College was a major sponsor of the National Trust's annual conference in Savannah in 1998 and celebrated its twentieth anniversary in 1999.

Mills B. Lane IV, who died in October 2001, conducted a preservation movement of his own beginning with the restoration of his house on Pulaski Square in 1971–72. He continued his father's interest in the enhancement of Bull Street by initiating and funding an improvement project that included repaving sidewalks with brick, tree planting, lighting and street furniture. The project was carried out under the direction of Historic Savannah Foundation. Mills Lane's knowledge of period architecture and of the correct scale and type of building to fit a specific location in Savannah meant that his restorations and new construction provided significant enhancements to the city. His reworking of his father's collection of ship models and placement of them in the Scarbrough House established a new level of excellence. Its beautiful garden, the largest and most luxuriant in downtown Savannah, is of special interest.

Today, Historic Savannah Foundation, with Mark McDonald as executive director, is continuing its vigil to assure that Savannah's city plan and heritage of eighteenth- and nineteenth-century architecture will endure in a vital environment that welcomes appropriate new construction in the twenty-first century.

We have lived in Savannah all our lives, have walked in its squares, and have been entertained in houses that are now museums. Through the years we have done what we could to influence appropriate change and are gratified that the city retains much of its beauty and its sophisticated, old-world elegance.

As we conclude, we also look toward the future. Savannah has seven districts on the National Register of Historic Places, and at this writing, Beth Reiter is working on an eighth nomination. The number of visitors from throughout the world who enjoy walking along Savannah's riverfront and through the magnificent squares in the National Landmark District continues to increase. We are conscious of the fragility of this area, realizing that it derives its excellence from the discipline of Oglethorpe's plan and architectural heritage.

It is our hope that preservationists, planners and city officials will always value Savannah's internationally acclaimed city plan as well as the historic structures, all of which give validity to its unique history as the nation's thirteenth English colony. Although it is important that new buildings respect Savannah's human scale and are constructed of materials that blend well with the historic buildings, the essential balance between the old and new could be lost if demolition of historic buildings is allowed to continue. We believe it is a critical necessity that the city plan and the remaining historic buildings in the National Landmark District are recognized as irreplaceable and invaluable assets.

Emma and Lee Adler on their front porch at 425 Bull Street, Monterey Square, Savannah, 1978.

Massie School, 1856-present, designed by architect John S. Norris, is owned and operated by the Savannah–Chatham County Public Schools. Its heritage education program has received state and national recognition.

Joan Mondale (fourth from left) visited Massie's exhibit on Savannah's architectural styles. Sarah Parsons pointed out some European influences on Savannah's historic buildings. At left are Emma Adler and Saxon Bargeron, members of the Friends of Massie committee. Second from right, Lee Adler talked with Ron Etheridge, superintendent of schools.

Celebrating Georgia's 250th Anniversary, February 12, 1983, the Georgia Day Procession assembled at Forsyth Park. Fourteen thousand elementary school children from across the State of Georgia walked down Bull Street to City Hall to be greeted by the Mayor of Savannah and dignitaries.

A Victorian district property before and after rehabilitation.

Rita Jones, of Savannah Landmark Rehabilitation Project, proclaimed the 300 Block of East Anderson Street Rousakis Row in honor of Savannah's Mayor, John Rousakis.

The Victorian district became another major preservation success.

Elizabeth (Beth) Lattimore Reiter, past Assistant Director of Historic Savannah Foundation, now Preservation Officer for the City of Savannah, lectured during Savannah's Neighborhood Action Conference in 1977.

James Biddle, President, National Trust for Historic Preservation, also took part in the Neighborhood Action Conference.

Lee Adler and Nancy Hanks, chair of the National Endowment for the Arts, conferred during the Neighborhood Action Conference.

The founding of the Savannah College of Art and Design (SCAD) in 1979 was the springboard for a second wave of significant preservation in the National Historic District.

The Henry Street School, 115 West Henry Street, was designed by G. L. Norman in 1892. The school was closed in 1983 and was later purchased by SCAD for use as classrooms.

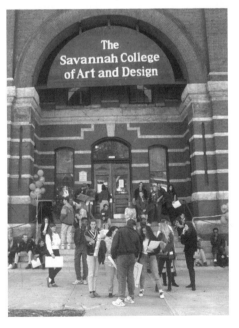

The Savannah College of Art and Design has restored more than fifty buildings in downtown Savannah. Two examples are the Old County Jail (left) and the Henry Street School (right).

The National Trust Annual Conference was held in Savannah in October, 1998. From left are Nancy Campbell, National Trust Chair, of New York; Westley W. Law, historian and preservationist, of Savannah; Lee Adler; and Richard Moe, President, National Trust for Historic Preservation.

HISTORIC PRESERVATION IN SAVANNAH, GEORGIA: A CHRONOLOGY

1857

Mary Telfair bequeaths her mansion designed by William Jay to the Georgia Historical Society. The building opens in 1886 as the Telfair Academy of Arts and Sciences.

1921

The Society for the Preservation of Parks is formed and successfully halts a "progressive" plan to cut streets through Savannah's squares.

1928

The Andrew Low House on Lafayette Square is purchased by the National Society of Colonial Dames in the State of Georgia for use as headquarters.

1930s

Williams Jay's Habersham House on Orleans Square and the Wetter House on Oglethorpe Avenue at West Broad Street are demolished.

1934

A Historic American Buildings Survey (HABS) project records important buildings through photographs and measured drawings.

Henry Ford razes Henry McAlpin's Hermitage, an imposing plantation house on the Savannah River, and uses the bricks to construct a mansion at Richmond Hill on the Ogeechee River. Union Camp Paper Corporation builds its plant on the Hermitage site.

The Montgomery Street Squares are cut through to ease the flow of north-south traffic.

1935

Mayor Thomas Gamble creates The Savannah Commission for the Preservation of Landmarks.

1940s

Alida Harper Fowlkes restores the house of James Habersham, Jr. (1789) on Reynolds Square for use as a restaurant, The Pink House.

Mrs. Marmaduke Floyd restores an old tavern on East Broad Street and christens it The Pirates' House.

The Green-Meldrim House is saved by the Society for the Preservation of Landmarks founded by Walter Charlton Hartridge.

Mr. and Mrs. Hansell Hillyer reclaim the ten-acre tract laid out by General Oglethorpe as an experimental garden (the Trustees Garden area) surrounding the gas works, and restore buildings owned by The Savannah Gas Company, of which Mr. Hillyer is president.

1951

Miss Margaret (Meta) Thomas bequeaths her house, the Owens-Thomas house, to the Telfair Academy.

1953

The birthplace of Juliette Gordon Low on the northeast corner of Oglethorpe Avenue and Bull Street is purchased by the National Board of the Girl Scouts.

1954

The City Market (1888) is demolished to be replaced by a parking garage built by the city.

1955

Historic Savannah Foundation receives its charter as a non-profit organization dedicated to developing a long-range plan of preservation and restoration. The first general membership meeting is held November 9, 1955 in the ballroom of the DeSoto Hotel.

The Davenport House is purchased by Historic Savannah Foundation with assistance from Walter Charlton Hartridge, chief advisor to the organization.

1957

The Lachlan McIntosh House (1770) on East Oglethorpe Avenue is saved and held for resale.

1958

The Francis Stone House (1830) on East State Street across from the Davenport House is saved, restored, and, through Fred Wessels, is leased to the Unitarian congregation.

The Junior League of Savannah contributes $3,000 for the consulting services of Carl Feiss, F.A.I.A. Mr. Feiss recommends a professional inventory of the 2.2-square-mile area which developed from 1733 to 1856.

Emmett Park is saved from conversion to a parking lot through the efforts of Historic Savannah and the Trustees Garden Club.

1959

Marshall Row (1854), Oglethorpe Avenue between Abercorn and Lincoln Streets, is saved by four individuals acting for Historic Savannah Foundation: Albert Stoddard, President, Lee Adler II, Karl Roebling and Dr. J. Harry Duncan. Mr. Stoddard emphasizes that the hope is to "put the buildings into the hands of people who will restore them…Profit is not the aim of the investment."

1961

Historic Savannah Foundation's sixth annual meeting is held at Telfair Academy. Lee Adler is incoming president. Emphasis is placed on the fact that "in Savannah preservation goes hand in hand with economic progress." Plans to reestablish a tourist and convention bureau in the Chamber of Commerce are unveiled. The *Savannah Morning News* has assisted in developing a slide lecture which shows that Knoxville, Tennessee (pop. 132,000) does a million-dollar tourist business. A panel including Malcolm Bell, Jr., Charles F. Wood and Albert Stoddard and moderated by Mayor Malcolm Maclean follows the slide lecture.

The Mongin House (1797) is moved to the southeast trust lot on Warren Square, and restored by Mr. and Mrs. John W. Carswell.

The Davenport House becomes headquarters of Historic Savannah Foundation. Mrs. Nightingale McKinnon, Trustee, begins her long and dedicated service as chair of restoration and curator of the museum house.

Armstrong College plans to tear down important buildings on Gaston Street and in the Monterey Square area, as well as Gordon Row.

The important house at 205 E. York Street (1854) is purchased and resold to David Morrison who locates his office in the building.

1963

The Union Station on West Broad Street is demolished and replaced by the entrance of Interstate 16 into the city.

Eight buildings called Troup Trust are purchased for $27,500. The city, through the Housing Authority, launches the first urban conservation program in the Southeast, making mortgage money competitive with that available to a suburban community.

The Sturgis House (1819) on Reynolds Square is purchased and held for resale for a number of years before purchase by Morris Newspapers for its headquarters.

18 East Oglethorpe is saved, stabilizing the important block of the Juliette Low Birthplace.

1964

A revolving fund is established. The Savannah Foundation provides $75,000 on a matching basis. Historic Savannah raises $125,000. [The fund is called "revolving" because the properties purchased by the Foundation are to be resold and the original outlays recovered to be used again for other properties. It is recognized that resales may be at a loss. This deficit is considered the contribution of the Foundation to the cultural heritage and urban vitality of the city. The basic reason for the Foundation's existence is to take the financial burden of showing the way to practical modern use of important buildings.]

The Foundation works to improve lighting and surfacing of River Street.

1965

Reid Williamson is hired as Executive Director. The Pulaski Square/West Jones Street area redevelopment project is launched. Historic Savannah options properties in this 15-acre area and holds them for resale to individuals.

The Cluskey buildings (1850s), known as the courthouse annex between Drayton and Abercorn on York Street, are purchased and later resold and restored for use as offices. The Turner House (1880s) on Lafayette Square is saved after negotiations with the Catholic Diocese.

The first annual Georgia Day celebration takes place in Washington Square. Alexander A. Lawrence is speaker and Norris Pindar portrays James Edward Oglethorpe.

The *McCaskey Report*, by Thomas McCaskey, Travel Director, Colonial Williamsburg, reveals Savannah as a potential "goldmine" for the tourist industry. This report is commissioned by Historic Savannah Foundation and the Chamber of Commerce.

The Davenport Trophy is established to be awarded to outstanding preservationists not necessarily on an annual basis. The first recipient is Hansell Hillyer, Past President of HSF, for significant work in area restoration and for devising the plan to raise money for the revolving fund.

1966

A pilot project in commercial restoration is undertaken in the 100 block of West Congress Street.

The U. S. Department of the Interior designates the 2.2-square-mile area inventoried by Historic Savannah Foundation as the nation's largest urban National Historic Landmark District.

The Scarbrough House is purchased. Mrs. Craig Barrow gives her share to Historic Savannah and the two remaining interests are acquired. The house is put into the hands of a new organization, the Scarbrough Foundation.

The Junior League contributes $7,500 toward the salary of Historic Savannah Foundation's director for two years and $5,000 a year for two years toward the publication of the foundation's inventory. Two League members are to serve on the Foundation's Steering Committee and five members on its Executive Committee.

The DeSoto Hotel is destroyed, to be replaced by a Citizens and Southern Bank building and a Hilton hotel.

Antiques magazine devotes its March issue to Savannah's restoration movement.

1967

Historic Savannah Foundation purchases six properties owned by Armstrong College in a lump sum of $235,000, March 1.

1968

Historic Preservation Plan, criteria for new construction in the Historic District, is published by the Department of Housing and Urban Development. It is the work of Paul Muldawer.

After more than six years of work, Historic Savannah's professional inventory is published in a volume entitled *Historic Savannah*. The publication is made possible by the Junior League and the Wormsloe Foundation.

The National Trust for Historic Preservation holds its largest annual conference to date in Savannah. Nine hundred delegates attend.

1969

John Fisher-Smith, Chair, American Institute of Architects, visits Savannah to advise regarding high-rise construction on the riverfront west of City Hall.

Save the Bay, Inc. is formed to protest high-rise construction on the riverfront.

1972

Mills B. Lane IV restores 208 West Harris Street on Pulaski Square.

Historic Savannah Foundation undertakes restoration of the William Scarbrough House.

Historic Zoning Legislation passes by vote of 3 to 1 in public referendum.

Reid Williamson leaves; DeCoursey McIntosh becomes Executive Director, Historic Savannah Foundation.

1973

The Victorian District is listed on the National Register of Historic Places.

1974

Savannah Landmark Rehabilitation Project is incorporated as a non-profit entity.

1975

HAER team records the Central of Georgia Railroad Shop Complex.

1976

Massie School is listed on the National Register of Historic Places, April 13.

Central of Georgia Railroad, Savannah Depot and Train Shed is designated a National Historic Landmark by the Secretary of the Interior.

The Scarbrough House restoration is completed.

1977

Savannah's newly revitalized Riverfront Plaza is dedicated to Mayor John P. Rousakis, June 3.

Savannah Landmark holds a national conference bringing 400 participants from 38 states.

The Heritage Education program is launched at Massie with Sarah Parsons as teacher.

1978

May Day in Calhoun Square is revived as an annual festival by Massie's Heritage Education program.

First Lady Rosalyn Carter visits the Savannah Landmark project.

The annual Georgia Day Celebration's schools program is coordinated through the Massie Center.

The Central of Georgia Railroad Complex receives National Landmark designation.

1979

The Savannah College of Art and Design is founded by Richard and Paula Rowan, opening at the Guard's Armory with 79 students enrolled.

The Historic American Buildings Survey, National Park Service, documents the Victorian District.

Savannah Landmark becomes a limited partner with Cranston Companies of Ohio, enabling it to receive an acquisition loan from the Ford Foundation.

1981

Massie's Heritage Education program is presented at the annual conference of the National Trust for Historic Preservation in Washington, DC.

1982

Savannah Landmark and the City of Savannah receive a National Recognition Award from the U. S. Department of Housing and Urban Development.

The Savannah–Chatham County Public Schools become co-sponsors of the Georgia Heritage Celebration.

1986

Elizabeth (Beth) Lattimore Reiter is hired as Historic Preservation Officer by the City of Savannah.

1987

The Lucas Theater is saved; the Lucas Theatre for the Arts, Inc., a non-profit entity, is formed to guide the restoration.

The Massie Heritage Center receives a Governor's Award in the Humanities.

1991

Mills B. Lane IV gains possession of the Scarbrough House.

1994

Savannah's City Plan, Monuments and Public Spaces is one of two nominations from the USA to UNESCO's World Heritage List.

The Savannah College of Art and Design receives an Honor Award from the National Trust for Historic Preservation.

1997

The City of Savannah adopts an ordinance prepared by Christopher Chadbourne of Boston to protect the historic fabric of the National Historic District.

The Ships of the Sea Museum opens at the Scarbrough House. Mark McDonald becomes Executive Director of Historic Savannah Foundation.

1998

The National Trust for Historic Preservation holds its annual conference in Savannah. There are 2,500 participants.

LEADERS OF HISTORIC PRESERVATION IN SAVANNAH, GEORGIA

FOUNDERS, HISTORIC SAVANNAH FOUNDATION

Elinor Grunsfeld Adler
Katharine Judkins Clark
Anna Colquitt Hunter
Lucy Barrow McIntire
Dorothy Ripley Roebling
Nola McEvoy Roos
Jane Adair Wright

Walter Charlton Hartridge, mentor to Founders

EXECUTIVE DIRECTORS, HISTORIC SAVANNAH FOUNDATION

Pekoe Floyd
J. Reid Williamson, Jr.
Decoursey McIntosh
John Hayes
Neil Horstmann
Stephanie Churchill
Mark McDonald

PRESIDENTS, HISTORIC SAVANNAH FOUNDATION

Anna Colquitt Hunter (1955-1956)
Jack Rauers (1956-1958)
H. Hansell Hillyer (1958-1959)
Albert H. Stoddard (1959-1961)
Leopold Adler II (1961-1963)
Walter C. Scott (1963-1964
Leopold Adler II (1964-1968)
Robert D. Gunn (1968-1969)
Walter Hartridge II (1969-1970)
Dale E. Critz, Jr. (1970-1971)
Katherine E. Cobb (1971-1973)
Elizabeth A. Lee (1973-1975)
J. Wiley Ellis (1975-1976)
John E. Cay III (1976-1977)
Arnold Tenenbaum (1977-1979)
Elizabeth C. Sprague (1979-1981)
John Allen (1981-1983)
Jeanne M. Garlington (1983-1984
Robert S. Glenn, Jr. (1984-1986)
G. Kennedy Matthews (1986-1988)
Joseph A. Webster, Jr. (1988-1991)
Donna Butler (1991-1993)
Lee C. Mundell (1993-1995)
Lawrence B. Lee (1995-1997)
Susan Rites Myers (1997-1999)
Graham Sadler (1999-2001)
Helen Downing (2001-2003)

RECIPIENTS OF THE DAVENPORT TROPHY

The Davenport Trophy is presented by Historic Savannah Foundation to individuals or organizations that have contributed substantially to the purpose of Historic Savannah. Named for the house whose rescue was the Foundation's charter project and *raison d'être*, the trophy is not given every year, but rather when a truly significant effort is made in behalf of the Foundation's commitment to historic preservation.

1965	H. Hansell Hillyer
1966	Mr. and Mrs. Mills B. Lane, Jr.
1968	Mr. and Mrs. Leopold Adler II
1969	Junior League of Savannah, Inc.
1973	Katherine Eaton Cobb
1975	Elizabeth Andrews Lee
1978	Ethelyn Nightingale McKinnon
1980	Ann Wenner Osteen
1982	Albert Henry Stoddard
1983	Trustees Garden Club
1989	Elizabeth Lattimore Reiter
1993	Marjorie McKinnon Simpson
1995	Mary Helen Jones Ray
1996	Wesley Wallace Law
1998	Mills B. Lane IV
2000	Claire Duane Ellis
	Cornelia Rankin Groves
2002	Scott W. Smith

CHAIRS OF THE GEORGIA HERITAGE CELEBRATION

1965	S. Joseph Ward, Jr.
1966	Mrs. Robert Bahr (Mary Ann)
1967	Mrs. Audrey D. Rhangos (now Mrs. Richard Platt)
1968	Mr. & Mrs. Walter Hartridge II (Connie)
1969	Mrs. Wayne Cunningham (Sissy)
1970	Mr. & Mrs. Charles Tallman (Rosalie)
1971	Mrs. Rodney Hartmann
1972	Dr. & Mrs. Rodney Hartmann
1973	Mrs. J. Lawrence Dunn (Celia)
1974	Mrs. Edward H. Downing (Helen)
1975	Mrs. Walt Parmer
1976	Mrs. Emerson Ham (Mary)
1977	Mrs. Donald Harwood (Joan)
1978	Mrs. Alexandra D. Saunders
1979	Mrs. Heyward Gignilliat (Joy)
1981	Mrs. John Jurgenson (Ann)
1982	Mrs. Leamon Holliday (Julia)
1983	Sesquicentennial Celebration
	Mrs. Lee Adler II (Emma), local
	Dr. Preston Russell, state
1984	Mrs. George Oelschig (Shirley)
1985	Mrs. Peter Smyth (Rencie)
1986	Mrs. Richard Middleton (Dee)
1987	Mrs. Jerry Stuber (Charlotte)
1988	Mrs. Joseph Howard (Caroline)
1989	Mrs. Ralph Kennickell, Jr. (Mary Lawrence)
1990	Ms. Virginia Hall
1991	Ms. Kay Dowell
1992	Ms. Jan Brown
1993-94	Ms. Ann Smith
1995-96	Ms. Ann Smith
1997	Ms. Monica McGoldrick
1998	Mrs. Gary Wisenbaker (Jeannie)
1999	Mrs. Camille O'Neill Farrow
2000	Dr. Barbara Heuer
2001	Ms. Swann Siler
2002	Ms. Lisa White
2003	Judge Louisa Abbot